AUDIENCE ANALYSIS

Dedicated to the survivors of
Com. 625 Audience Analysis
at the A.S.C.,
University of Pennsylvania, 1971-72

AUDIENCE ANALYSIS

DENIS McQUAIL

SAGE Publications
International Educational and Professional Publisher
Thousand Oaks   London   New Delhi

For information:

SAGE Publications, Inc.
2455 Teller Road
Thousand Oaks, California 91320
E-mail: order@sagepub.com

SAGE Publications Ltd.
6 Bonhill Street
London EC2A 4PU
United Kingdom

SAGE Publications India Pvt. Ltd.
M-32 Market
Greater Kailash I
New Delhi 110 048 India

Printed in the United States of America

Library of Congress Cataloging-in-Publication Data

McQuail, Denis.
    Audience analysis/by Denis McQuail.
      p. cm.
    Includes bibliographical references and index.
    ISBN 0-7619-1001-8 (cloth: acid-free paper).
    ISBN 0-7619-1002-6 (pbk.: acid-free paper).
    1. Mass media—Audiences. I. Title.
P96.A83M39 1997   97-4855
302.23—dc21

97 98 99 00 01 02 03 10 9 8 7 6 5 4 3 2 1

Acquiring Editor:	Margaret Seawell
Editorial Assistant:	Renée Piernot
Production Editor:	Astrid Virding
Production Assistant:	Denise Santoyo
Typesetter/Designer:	Marion S. Warren
Cover Designer:	Candice Harman
Print Buyer:	Anna Chin

CONTENTS

PREFACE

This short book has been a long time in gestation. By one reckoning its origins lie in now long-forgotten Ph.D. research into the audience for television plays on British television in the early 1960s. But the topic has been a matter of continuous curiosity to me ever since. The audience currently appears to hold the key to several mysteries surrounding the way the mass media work and even to the very survival of "mass communication" as we know it. At the same time, the search for the key to the mystery of the audience itself is still under way and it has been hard to keep up with new developments in thinking since this particular book was conceived, at the start of the 1990s. I hope it helps to clear the ground for what is an important ongoing enterprise, especially at a time when new forms of audience are emerging which are challenging older theory.

I am grateful to Jack McLeod and Steve Chaffee for inviting me to write the book originally and especially to the latter for his rigorous editing and advice. In thinking about this preface, I was reminded of the fact that studying the audience was also great fun, especially in the often zany company of Ray Brown and Jay Blumler. For us the personal human gratifications of studying the audience far outweighed the uses. I suspect the same applies to most audience behavior, although it is a hypothesis which remains to be tested. Finally, I am grateful for the very expeditious and helpful way in which the publisher has turned a manuscript into a printed book. In this particular case, I am expecting that audience utlility will exceed gratification.

—Denis McQuail
Amsterdam

ONE

A CONCEPT
WITH A HISTORY

The Audience Problem

The word *audience* has long been familiar as the collective term for the "receivers" in the simple sequential model of the mass communication process (source, channel, message, receiver, effect) that was deployed by pioneers in the field of media research (see, e.g., Schramm, 1954). There is an established discourse in which "audience" simply refers to the readers of, viewers of, listeners to one or other media channel or of this or that type of content or performance. It also designates one branch of the subject matter in the study of mass communication and one main field of empirical research. It is a term that is understood by media practitioners and theorists alike and it has entered into everyday usage, recognized by media users as an unambiguous description of themselves.

Nevertheless, beyond commonsense usage, there is much room for differences of meaning, misunderstandings, and theoretical conflicts. The problems surrounding the concept stem mainly from the fact that a single and simple word is being applied to an increasingly diverse and complex reality, open to alternative and competing theoretical formulations. One commentator

1

has gone as far as to suggest that "what is occurring is the breakdown of the *referent* for the word audience in communication research from both the humanities and the social sciences" (Biocca, 1988a, p. 103). In other words, we keep the familiar word, but the thing itself is disappearing.

The audience for most mass media is not usually observable, except in fragmentary or indirect ways. Hence the term *audience* has an abstract and debatable character, much as with other apparently simple concepts in the social sciences such as *society* or *public opinion*. The reality to which the term refers is also diverse and constantly changing. The term *audience* can, for instance, be applied equally to the set of readers of early 18th-century novels and to subscribers to late 20th-century satellite television services, although these two phenomena are very different. This illustrates the strength and appeal of a simple concept but also draws attention to pitfalls if we have no clear and agreed understanding of what the term means.

Audiences are both a product of social context (which leads to shared cultural interests, understandings, and information needs) and a response to a particular pattern of media provision. Often they are both at the same time, as when a medium sets out to appeal to the members of a social category or the residents of a certain place. Media use also reflects broader patterns of time use, availability, lifestyle, and everyday routines.

An audience can thus be defined in different and overlapping ways: by *place* (as in the case of local media); by *people* (as when a medium is characterized by an appeal to a certain age group, gender, political belief, or income category); by the particular type of *medium* or *channel* involved (technology and organization combined); by the *content* of its messages (genres, subject matter, styles); by *time* (as when one speaks of the "daytime" or the "prime-time" audience, or an audience that is fleeting and short term compared to one that endures). These opening remarks are sufficient to illustrate how this simple term embodies many ambiguities.

History of the Audience

The early origins of today's media audience lie in public theatrical and musical performances as well as in the games and spectacles of ancient times. Our earliest notions of audience are of a physical gathering in a certain place. A Greek or Roman city would have a theater or arena and it was no doubt preceded by informal gatherings for similar events and for religious or state occasions. The Greco-Roman audience had many features that are familiar today, including:

- Planning and *organization* of viewing and listening, as well as of the performances themselves
- Events with a *public* and "popular" character
- *Secular* (thus not religious) content of performance—for entertainment, education, and vicarious emotional experience
- *Voluntary,* individual acts of choice and attention
- *Specialization* of roles of authors, performers, and spectators
- Physical *locatedness* of performance and spectator experience

The audience, thus, as a set of spectators for public events of a secular kind, was already institutionalized more than two thousand years ago. It had its own customs, rules, and expectations about the time, place, and content of performances; conditions for admission; and so forth. It was typically an urban phenomenon, often with a commercial basis, and content varied according to social class and status. The more educated assembled for literary and musical works, while a larger public attended fights, races, games, comedies, and circuses.

Even this early audience was only one element in a larger institution that included professional writers, performers, producers, and entrepreneurs. The phenomenon of public display and entertainment attracted sponsorship as well as censorship and could serve political or religious ends. It was an object of moral and intellectual comment and subject to surveillance by authorities. In many other cultures around the world, similar institutions of public performance existed, although perhaps with a less clearly urban, secular, and individualistic character than in the Greco-Roman tradition.

Several features set the early form of audience apart from its modern media equivalent. Most important, the audience of classical times was localized in place and time. An audience occupied an "auditorium," a space in which to hear and see what was going on and to respond directly. This meant that the audience was necessarily small by modern standards (though it could number thousands). It was potentially active within itself and interactive with performers. Performances were always "live," in the fullest possible sense.

Such an audience had a potential collective life of its own, based on a common background and the shared experience of the moment. These conditions still prevail in many circumstances of public display and spectatorship today—in theaters and stadiums, for example. There has since been a proliferation of audience forms, but media technological inventions have also brought the social innovation of a new dominant form, one that retains some of the meaning of the early "audience," but which is no longer the same. It differs especially in being much larger, much more dispersed, individualized, and privatized.

The emergence of the mass media audience began mainly with the introduction of the printed book. This allowed effective communication *at a distance* in space and time and also privacy in use (see Kaufer & Carley, 1993). With the book came the new phenomenon of a dispersed *reading public*—a set of individuals choosing the same texts. The printing of books, starting in the mid-15th century, gradually led to an organized supply of nonreligious written texts that could be bought by individuals for their own instruction, entertainment, or enlightenment. It was late in the 16th century before one might sensibly speak of a reading public composed of individuals who could buy, read, and collect books for their private purposes. Reading publics tended to remain localized in cities and were circumscribed by social status and language (although there were translations early on). They were supplied by growing numbers of printer/publishers and authors and were sometimes supported by sponsors and patrons (Febvre & Martin, 1984).

The book was not the only print form involved. By the early 18th century, periodical magazines and newspapers were also likely to have regular followings. The expanding print media industry was commonly an object of censorship or regulation, for political and religious reasons. Before the 19th century inventions, which made printed media products cheap and plentiful, the "public" or audience for printed matter was already quite diversified and subject to divisions and social definitions, which have since been formalized in the categories of audience research. These have to do with differences of content and differences among people, especially in terms of class, status, and education. Reading preferences often overlapped with other social characteristics and locations just as they do now with film and electronic media.

A series of now familiar changes in technology and society fundamentally altered the nature of audiences, especially in respect of scale. Urbanization, rail transportation, improved technology of printing, increased literacy, and rising living standards had, by the end of the 19th century, transformed the cozy world of book and periodical production into large-scale industries serving millions at a time. The increased scale of media reach was also fueled by the growth of the advertising industry, which helped to finance cheap daily newspapers, popular magazines, and books. Along with larger scale came much more dispersal and differentiation of audience activity.

The first social scientific concept of the audience emerged after one other significant step in media development had been taken—the invention of film and the cinema form of distribution (Jowett & Linton, 1980). The moving pictures shown in public halls restored the original *locatedness* of reception, in continuity with the theater rather than the printing press. The cinema also created the first genuine "mass audience," in the sense of large-scale reception of the identical message or performance. Millions of ordinary people came to enjoy the same mediated emotional and learning experiences. The film audience could not really *interact* with its object of attention, but its members could interact with each other. Aside from content, the main difference from the theater was that there was no live performance (aside from the musical accompaniment) and the show was always and everywhere the same.

Starting in the 1920s, broadcasting initiated another phase of audience history in which the creation of new kinds of audience based on *technology* became a major goal of expanding and profitable media industries. Competition for audiences increasingly became a matter of competing equipment, as seen again more recently with the rivalry among cable, satellite, and broadcast distribution and between competing video and audio recording systems.

The case of broadcasting also helps to illustrate another of the main early preoccupations of media audience theory and research. Broadcasting was first of all a technology of distribution, developed out of radio-telephony, which only gradually acquired its own distinctive forms (Williams, 1974). It was initially a "hardware" industry rather than a communication service. Its aim was to acquire listeners and stimulate a demand for the distribution service. Once this was in place, receiving sets could be sold and the basis for further technological development was laid. For the first time (although the telephone and phonograph records could offer precedents), an audience could be defined as consisting of those who possessed the reception equipment.

Television broadcasting, which rapidly eclipsed radio and the cinema, and overshadowed the popular book and newspaper press, accentuated concern about several mass-like characteristics of audiences. Television's simultaneity of impact was much greater and affected larger numbers. Greater, too, was its uniformity and the perishability of its content (compared with print media, certainly). Early writing about television emphasized its addictive pull, its ubiquitous invasion of social and cultural space, and its seeming passivity and emptiness as a leisure-time activity (e.g., Himmelweit, Vince, & Oppenheim, 1958; Schramm, Lyle, & Parker, 1961; Steiner, 1963).

In addition, the privatization of media experience was increased, or so it seemed. Though people might read their newspapers in public places and "go out" to the cinema as a social event with friends, television viewing was indisputably a private affair. The audience for what was usually a limited supply of television (compared to today's abundance) seemed to be even more of a mass phenomenon—large, anonymous, addicted, passive. The audience for television, as for radio, was notable for yet another reason: Unlike previous media audiences, it was largely outside the range of direct observation and record.

The Audience as a Mass

Although many observers commented on the amazing new possibilities for reaching so many disparate people so quickly by the press, film, or radio, the first theoretical formulation of the media audience concept stemmed from a wider consideration of the changing nature of social life in modern society. A member of the early Chicago School of sociology, Herbert Blumer (1939), first provided an explicit framework in which the audience could be exemplified as a new form of collectivity made possible by the conditions of modern societies. He called this phenomenon a "mass" and differentiated it from older social forms—especially the group, the crowd, and the public.

In the small *group,* all of its members know and interact with each other within certain social and physical boundaries. They are aware of their common membership and share similar values. The structure of group relationships is clear and persists over time. The *crowd* is a larger unit, although spatially restricted. It is also temporary and rarely re-forms with the same composition. It may have a sense of shared identity and "mood," but it is essentially unstable and acts irrationally and on the basis of impulse. According to Blumer (1946), the crowd "is a non-cultural group, so likewise is it a non-moral group" (p. 174). The *"public"* is a product of modern conditions, especially when seen as an element in the institution of democratic politics. It consists of a set of people who engage freely in the discussion of some public issue, with a view to advancing some opinion, interest, policy, or proposal for change.

The *mass* was seen as a product of the new conditions of modern industrial urban society, especially its largeness of scale, anonymity, and rootlessness.

It is typically a very large aggregate of detached individuals, anonymous to each other, but with their attention converging on some object of interest that is outside their immediate personal environment or control. As with the crowd, the mass lacks any organization, stable structure, rules, or leadership. Unlike the crowd, it has no will or means to act for itself and it has no fixed location.

This concept of a mass seemed to capture several essential features of the audiences attracted to the commercial newspaper and the cinema. The audience was large and widely dispersed; its members did not and could not know each other; its composition was always shifting and it lacked any sense of self-identity, due to its dispersion and heterogeneity; it was not governed by any norms or rules; it appeared not to act for itself, but to be acted on from outside. Just as its own internal relations were impersonal, so also were the relations between the audience and the mass media. The audience cannot easily "talk back" to the producers and senders of mass media messages. The communicative relationship involved is typically calculative and nonmoral, with no real commitment or attachment on either side. There is also often a large *social* distance between a more powerful, expert, or prestigeful media source and the audience member.

This view of the mass audience is less a description of reality than an accentuation of features typical of conditions of mass production and distribution of news and entertainment. When used by early commentators, the term generally had a pejorative connotation, reflecting Western values of individualism and a pessimistic view of modern industrial society, by contrast with an image of a more communal and satisfying way of life. Calling an audience a mass reflected fears of depersonalization, irrationality, manipulation, and of a general decline in cultural or moral standards. As later critics have pointed out, the real problem was not the existence of "the masses," but the tendency to treat people as if they were masses (Williams, 1961).

Rediscovery of the
Audience as a Group

The reality of people's experience of mass print and film has always been very diverse. While impersonality, anonymity, and vastness of scale might describe the phenomenon in general, much actual audience experience is personal, small scale, and integrated into social life and familiar ways. Many media operate in local environments and are embedded in local cultures. Because most people make their own media choices freely, they do not typically feel manipulated by remote powers. The social interaction that develops around media use helps people to incorporate it into everyday life as a friendly rather than an alienating presence.

There was a significant turning point in the history of mass communication theory, during the 1940s and 1950s (Delia, 1987), when the atomistic conception of a mass audience was challenged by researchers (see especially Katz & Lazarsfeld, 1955). Research hailed the "rediscovery of the group," finding evidence that it had never really disappeared, even in the seemingly unfavorable conditions of the large industrial city (Janowitz, 1952). Actual audiences were shown to consist of many overlapping networks of social relations based on locality and common interests, and the "mass" media were incorporated into these networks in different ways. The communal and social group character of audiences was restored to conceptual prominence (e.g., Janowitz, 1952; Merton, 1949).

Research into media effects was, from the 1950s onward, also obliged to take into account the fact that opinions, attitudes, and behaviors are much more influenced by one's social environment than by persuasive appeals via the mass media. The notions of "personal influence" and "opinion leaders" presumed a situation in which contact with the media was mediated by a variety of social relationships that served to guide, filter, and interpret media experience. This applied not only to political and commercial persuasion, but also to learning about news events, which was also shown to be significantly related to having personal contacts (Greenberg, 1964; Rosengren, 1973).

The Audience as Market

However one interprets the early history of broadcasting, there is no doubt that the radio and television audience rapidly developed into an important consumer market for hardware and software. At first sight, the widely used expression "media market" might seem to offer a more objective alternative to other, more value-laden terms to describe the audience phenomenon. As the media have become bigger business, the term *market* has gained in currency. It can designate regions served by media, social-demographic categories, or the actual or potential consumers of particular media services or products. It can be defined as an "aggregate of actual or potential consumers of media services and products, with a known social-economic profile."

Although the market concept is a pragmatic and useful one for media industries and for analyzing media economics, it can also be problematic and it is not really value-free. It links sender and receiver in a "calculative" rather than a normative or social relationship, as a cash transaction between producer and consumer rather than a communication relationship. It ignores the internal relations among consumers, since these are of little interest to service providers. It privileges socioeconomic criteria and focuses on media *consumption* rather than reception.

Effective communication and the quality of audience experience are of secondary importance in market thinking. The significance of audience experience for the wider public sphere is also de-emphasized. The view of the audience as market is inevitably the view "from the media" (especially of their owners and managers) and within the terms of the media industries' discourse. People in audiences do not normally have any awareness of themselves as belonging to markets, and the market discourse in relation to the audience is implicitly manipulative.

New Media and the
Future of the Audience

As a result of new media developments, four main changes have affected the audience (and ideas about it). First are the new possibilities for delivering television (and radio) broadcasting via cable and satellite. Supply had previously been limited by the range of terrestrial transmitters carrying a very few channels. The result has been a relative "abundance" of supply of audiovisual media and content and a greatly increased choice for many. Adding to this increased supply is an enlargement of reception possibilities as apparatus becomes cheaper. Much greater ease of message reproduction and distribution has also affected print media and various branches of the music industry.

A second change has been the rapid development of new ways of recording, storage, and retrieval of sound and pictures, now beginning to approach the ease and flexibility of print storage. These new possibilities are largely available to all media consumers. The video recorder and playback machine has had a considerable impact, because it shifts control of the timing of television or film reception from the sender to the receiver, thus increasing abundance and choice. Even the television remote-control device tends to increase choice, by making it easier to look for alternatives. Taken together, these changes are reducing the homogeneity and simultaneity of audience experience. As a result, there are more numerous and more fleeting audiences for television, and audience segmentation and fragmentation have been widely predicted.

A third change relates to the increased transnationalization of television flow, as a result of the worldwide growth of new services, the capacity for satellite transmission to cross national frontiers, and the greater import and export of film and television program content. While this trend has had more impact on countries other than the United States, which remains largely self-sufficient in media terms, there is an increased potential for very large, worldwide audiences to be recruited for events or spectacles of especial interest. We also see evidence of increased global marketing of media stars and media products. In smaller countries, especially, local or national audiences are less protected from global cultural influences.

The fourth innovation derives from the increasingly interactive capacity use of various media, as a result of computer-based systems. One-way systems become two-way or even multiple networks. The media user can acquire control of the information environment. The resulting interactive media networks have been welcomed by some as the basis for local community or for wider, interest-based, associations and "cyber-communities" (Jones, 1995; Rheingold, 1994). In principle, this would seem to run counter to the general trend of media history, restoring a human scale and individuality to mediated social communication, restoring the balance of power of the receiver at the periphery as against the dominant centralized sender. But it also increases the individuation of use and fragmentation of the mass audience. It is also still unclear how far the audience wants to be interactive.

In a fully decentralized network, the traditional concept of audience is hereby abolished or becomes a misnomer, replaced by countless sets of consumers of information services of unlimited variety. If this should happen, it certainly means the "breakdown of the referent," as noted earlier. The concept of mass medium is equally threatened, because no one will be obliged to accept the same package of information at the same time as anyone else. Arguably, without a mass medium there is no single, collective, audience— only chance similarities of patterns of media use. However, while this is a theoretical possibility it is not yet a reality. The most far-reaching technical possibilities seem more to have extended rather than to have replaced the older patterns of "audience behavior." Audiences can now be larger and more "massive" than ever before.

This serves as a reminder that audiences are not just a product of technology, but also of social life. There are continuing social forces that generate the formation of audiences. It is the same forces, rather than the media, that will determine whether or not we find ourselves in an atomized and alienated world. The possibility of entering an interactive utopia is also as much dependent on social factors as on technological possibilities.

Conclusion

This book has a number of aims. One is to explore the issues raised above and to report whatever light communication theory and research have been able to shed. Another is to describe and explain the main branches of audience research and different schools of thought about the audience. Third, various subconcepts and models developed as tools of audience analysis are explained. Finally, the book will try to assess the meaningfulness and relevance of the audience concept, in the light of predictions of the decline of mass media and the demise of the audience as we have historically known it.

TWO

Thε Audiεncε in Communication Thεory and Rεsεarch

Critical Perspectives

Perceptions of the audience have often been influenced by negative views about mass media in general and have ranged from simple prejudice and snobbery to sophisticated exercises in media analysis. The first category is exemplified by the view that equates large media audiences with the "lowest common denominator" of taste and that assumes that "mass culture," "low taste," and "mass audience" are more or less synonymous. This way of thinking has been described as an "ideology of mass culture" (Ang, 1985), according to which much popular entertainment is automatically condemned as inferior, and those who like it as lacking in taste and discrimination.

A more sophisticated critique of mass culture was mounted from the left of the ideological spectrum, especially from the perspective of the Marxist "Frankfurt School" in the 1940s and 1950s. The mass audience was pictured as the more or less helpless victims of manipulation and exploitation by capitalist media devoted to purveying "false consciousness," meaning essentially the loss of any sense of class identity and solidarity (for accounts see, e.g., Hart, 1991; Jay, 1973; Rosenberg & White, 1957). The victimized working classes were unable to defend themselves against propaganda and manipulation because of their lack of education and their experience of mindless and exhausting labor, from which mass culture, however unedifying, was a pleasant relief.

C. Wright Mills (1951, 1956), in his radical critique of American society in the 1950s, elaborated on the extreme dependence and vulnerability of the ordinary person in the face of the monopoly media and advertising industry. The media were attributed the power to create extreme dependence in respect of basic psychic needs for identity and self-realization. The way they were organized made it virtually impossible to answer back and the media could impose a "psychological illiteracy." According to Marcuse (1964), incorporation into the mass audience was part of the process of control and homogenization that led to a "one-dimensional society," meaning a society in which real differences of class interests were concealed without being resolved. Consumer and audience demands were interpreted in critical theory as "false needs" (artificially stimulated) whose satisfaction benefited only the ruling capitalist class.

The generation of media critics of the immediate post Second World War period were often populist and pro-democratic in their aims, but also pessimistic about the will and the capacity of the media audience to resist exploitation by the sophisticated new "consciousness industries." They believed in the possibility of redemption, but only if the capitalist system could be removed or reformed. The cultural critics of the succeeding generation, represented mainly in Britain by Hoggart (1957), Williams (1961), and Hall (1977) and in the United States by Gitlin (1978), Carey (1974, 1975, 1977), Newcomb (1976), and others, reinterpreted the predominant tastes and preferences of the "mass" audience in a positive way. They rejected the concept of mass and refused to equate popular culture with "low culture" (McGuigan, 1992). Popular culture was seen as different in kind from "high" culture rather than inferior, and best interpreted according to its local and particular meanings.

Even so, the main thrust of critique from the Left remained grounded in an attack on the commercial exploiters of more or less vulnerable media consumers. According to Gitlin (1978), the representation in communication research of the audience as active and resistant (as noted above) was itself largely an ideological move designed to obscure the continuing reality and to deflect the attack on monopolist, capitalist media. The school of audience research (especially the "uses and gratifications" approach) that emphasized the audience as being "in charge" of their media experience (see "The Behaviorist Tradition: Media Effects and Media Uses," this chapter) was also attacked for overstating the real autonomy of the audience (Elliott, 1974).

In an innovative and sophisticated move, the Canadian Dallas Smythe (1977) gave birth to the theory that audiences actually *work* for advertisers (thus, for their ultimate oppressors) by giving their free time to watch media, which labor is then packaged and sold by the media to advertisers as a new kind of "commodity." The whole system of commercial television and the press rests on this extraction of surplus value from an economically exploited audience. The same audience has to pay yet again for its media, by way of the extra cost added to the advertised goods. It was an ingenious and convincing piece of theorizing that revealed the mass audience phenomenon in quite a new light (see Jhally & Livant, 1986). It is plausible to suppose that the media need their audience more than audiences need their media, and there is also reason to view audience research as primarily a tool for the close control and management (call it manipulation) of media audiences.

A more recent critical view charges the media industry with routinely transforming the actual television audience into a piece of commercial information called "ratings" (Ang, 1991). Ratings are described as forming "the basis for the agreed-upon standard by which advertisers and network buy and sell the audience commodity" (p. 54). Ang reminds us that "watching television is an ongoing, day-to-day cultural practice engaged in by millions of people" and the "ratings discourse" serves to "capture and encompass the viewing practice of all these people in a singular, object-ified, streamlined construct of 'television audience.' " These comments essentially label the industry view of the audience as intrinsically dehumanizing and exploitative. Again, it reflects the view that commercial mass media are served by their audiences rather than vice versa.

Up to a point, critical theory does no more than put an extra interpretive gloss on views about the power of the media to hold and attract their audience. These ideas are much more widely held and also carry more "scientific" credentials. For instance, the still widely current media dependency theory of Ball-Rokeach and DeFleur (1976) is based on an assumption of audience submission to the media system as a normal condition of modern society. The cultural indicators theory of Gerbner and associates (Signorielli & Morgan, 1990) also presumes a degree of addictive power on the part of the medium of television. As we will see, there is a strong and continuing strand of judgmental attitudinizing with respect to audiences. Ideological critique, social concern, moralizing, and cultural pessimism are intermingled, and the more recent effort by the field of cultural studies to liberate the audience from these shackles has not fully succeeded (Ferguson & Golding, 1997; McGuigan, 1992).

Goals of Audience Research

Because the audience has always been a contested category, it is not surprising that the purposes of doing research into audiences are varied and often inconsistent. All research shares the general characteristic that it helps to "construct," "locate," or "identify" an otherwise amorphous, shifting, or unknowable social entity. But the methods used, the constructions of the audience arrived at, and the uses to which they are put all diverge considerably. Leaving aside the purposes of theory building, we can classify research goals in terms of the main uses to which information about the audience can be put. These include:

- accounting for sales (bookkeeping)
- measuring actual and potential reach for purposes of advertising
- manipulating and channeling audience choice behavior
- looking for audience market opportunities
- product testing and improving communication effectiveness
- meeting responsibilities to serve an audience
- evaluating media performance in a number of ways (e.g., to test allegations of harmful effects)

Perhaps the most fundamental division of purpose is that between media industry goals and those that take the perspective and "side" of the audience. Research can, as it were, represent the voice of the audience, or speak on its behalf. The goal of meeting responsibilities to the audience often guides research carried out by public broadcasters (e.g., Emmett, 1968). It is also represented by recent developments in the United States referred to as "public" or "civic" journalism (Rosen & Merritt, 1994). Newspapers, for instance, are urged to take better account, in selecting news, of the needs and interests of their own (usually local) readers through intensive and continuous research. Although it is not at all sure that audience research can ever truly serve the audience alone, we can provisionally view the different purposes of research as extending along a dimension ranging from AUDIENCE CONTROL to AUDIENCE AUTONOMY.

By far the greatest quantity of audience research belongs at the Control end of the spectrum, since this is what the industry wants and pays for (Beniger, 1986). Few of the results of industry research appear in the public domain and are consequently neglected in academic accounts of the audience. Despite this overall imbalance of research effort, the clearest line of development in audience theory has been a move away from the perspective of the media communicator and toward that of the receiver. Accounts of audience research have increasingly tended to emphasize the "rediscovery" of people and the notion of an active and obstinate audience in the face of attempted manipulation or persuasion.

Alternative Traditions of Research

Jensen and Rosengren (1990) distinguished five traditions of audience research that can be summarized as having to do with: effects; uses and gratifications; literary criticism; cultural studies; and reception analysis. For present purposes, it is convenient to deploy a somewhat more economical typology of audience research, by identifying three main variant approaches under the headings "structural," "behavioral," and "sociocultural." The first of these is not well covered by Jensen and Rosengren's scheme and the "literary criticism" heading is of little relevance here.

The Structural Tradition of Audience Measurement

The needs of media industries gave rise to the earliest and simplest kinds of research, which were designed to obtain reliable estimates of what were otherwise unknown quantities—especially the size and reach of radio audiences and the "reach" of print publications (the number of potential readers as opposed to the circulation or print-run). These data were essential to management, especially for gaining paid advertising. In addition to size, it was important to know about the social composition of audiences in basic terms—the who and where of the audience. These elementary needs gave rise to an immense industry interconnected with that of advertising and market research.

The structural approach is theoretically important because it can help to show the relation between the media system and individual media use (Weibull, 1985). For instance, choice is always limited by what is available in a given media market. It is also important in research on communication effects, as when opinion, attitude, or reported behavior data are interrelated with data about media use patterns and with demographic data. The amount and kind of media "exposure" is always a key variable in effects analysis. The structural approach can also be used to study the "flow" of an audience over time between different channels and content types (e.g., Barwise & Ehrenberg, 1988; Emmett, 1972). It can be used to establish typologies of viewers, listeners, and readers (e.g., Espé & Seiwert, 1986; McCain, 1986; Weiman, Wober, & Brosius, 1992) by relating media use behavior with relevant social background characteristics. Not least, it has a role to play in making media more publicly accountable. Audience surveys can measure the relative satisfaction or trust that different sectors of the media enjoy.

The Behaviorist Tradition: Media Effects and Media Uses

Early mass communication research was mainly preoccupied with media effects, especially on children and young people, and with an emphasis on potential harm (see Klapper, 1960). Nearly every serious effects study has also been an audience study, in which the audience is conceptualized as "exposed" to influence or impact, whether of a persuasive, learning, or behavioral kind. The typical effects model was a one-way process in which the audience was conceived as an unwitting target or a passive recipient of media stimuli.

Much early effects research followed the experimental approach, in which communication conditions (of content, channel, and reception) were manipulated in the search for general lessons about how better to communicate or to avoid harmful consequences. An early example was the wartime research program into film as a motivational and training tool for recruits

(Hovland, Lumsdaine, & Sheffeld, 1949). The appeal of, and response to, portrayals of violence and related phenomena in the media have mainly been investigated within this tradition. The Payne Fund studies into the effects of film on youth (e.g., Blumer, 1933) provide the first example of such research. Many studies of elections, beginning with Lazarsfeld, Berelson, and Gaudet's (1944) classic study of the U.S. 1940 presidential election have sought to relate audience behavior to voting behavior.

The second main type of "behavioral" audience research was in many ways a reaction to the model of direct effects. Media *use* was now central and the audience was viewed as a more or less active and motivated set of media users/consumers, who were "in charge" of their media experience, rather than passive "victims." Research focused on the origin, nature, and degree of motives for choice of media and media content. Audiences were also permitted to provide the definitions of their own behavior (see Blumler & Katz, 1974).

Pioneering examples can be found of research into the motives and selection patterns of audiences, mostly conducted in a social-psychological mode (e.g., Cantril & Allport, 1935, on the radio audience; Lazarsfeld & Stanton, 1949; Waples, Berelson, & Bradshaw, 1940, on reading). This tradition subsequently developed by way of many studies into mass media violence (see Comstock, Chaffee, Katzman, McCombs, & Roberts, 1978) and into the uses (positive as well as harmful) of mass media by children (Rosengren & Windahl, 1989; Schramm et al., 1961). A distinctive subtradition later crystallized out in the form of research into the motives for media choice and the perceived gratifications and uses of media (Blumler & Katz, 1974; Rosengren, Palmgreen, & Rayburn, 1985). The "uses and gratifications" approach is not strictly "behavioral," since its main emphasis is on the social origins of media gratifications and on the wider social functions of media, for instance in facilitating social contact and interaction or in reducing tension and anxiety.

The Cultural Tradition and Reception Analysis

The cultural studies tradition also occupies a borderland between social science and the humanities. It has been almost exclusively concerned with works of popular culture in contrast to an early literary tradition. It emphasizes media use as a reflection of a particular sociocultural context and as a process of giving meaning to cultural products and experiences. This school of research rejects both the stimulus-response model of effects and the notion of an all-powerful text or message. At first, attempts were made (e.g., Morley, 1980) to show that messages could be "read" or "decoded" quite variously by differently constituted social and cultural groups and also differently than intended by their originators. As decoding research merged into the general rise of media cultural studies in the 1980s, it became axiomatic to expect, and not too hard to prove, that most media messages were essentially "polysemic" (i.e., having multiple meanings) and open to several possible interpretations (Liebes & Katz, 1986, 1989, 1990).

The other main strand of the culturalist approach involves a view of media use as in itself a significant aspect of "everyday life." Media use practices can only be understood in relation to the particular social context and experience of a subcultural group (Bausinger, 1984). Media reception research emphasized the study of audiences as "interpretive communities" (Lindlof, 1988). This concept refers to shared outlook and modes of understanding, often arising out of shared social experiences.

Reception analysis is effectively the audience research arm of modern cultural studies, rather than an independent tradition. It strongly emphasizes the role of the "reader" in the "decoding" of media texts. It has generally had a consciously "critical" edge, in the terms discussed above, claiming for the audience a power to resist and subvert the dominant or hegemonic meanings offered by the mass media. It is characterized by the use of qualitative and ethnographic methods (Morley, 1992; Seiter, Borchers, Kreutzner, & Warth, 1989).

The main features of the culturalist (reception) tradition of audience research can be summarized as follows (though not all are exclusive to this approach):

- the media text has to be "read" through the perceptions of its audience, which constructs meanings and pleasures from the media texts offered (and these are never fixed or predictable)
- the very process of media use and the way in which it unfolds in a particular context are central objects of interest
- media use is typically situation-specific and oriented to social tasks that evolve out of participation in "interpretative communities"
- audiences for particular media genres often comprise separate "interpretative communities" that share much the same forms of discourse and frameworks for making sense of media
- audiences are never passive, nor are all their members equal, since some will be more experienced or more active fans than others
- methods have to be "qualitative" and deep, often ethnographic, taking account of content, act of reception, and context together (Lindlof, 1991)

It is fairly obvious that this tradition has little in common with either the structuralist or behaviorist approaches. Ang (1991) criticized the "mainstream" audience research tradition for adopting an "institutional" view that aims to produce commercial and institutional knowledge of an abstraction of the audience for purposes of control and manipulation. She argues that media institutions have no real interest in *knowing* their audiences, only in being able to prove there is one, by way of systems and techniques of measurement (e.g., "people meters") that convince their clients, but that can never begin to capture the true essence of "audiencehood." Behaviorist and psychological approaches may get nearer to the goal of describing the nature of audience experience but from the cultural perspective the outcomes of research remain abstract, individualized, and desiccated renderings that can only lend themselves to manipulative purposes. The three traditions are summarily compared in Table 2.1.

There are some indications of increasing convergence in research approaches (Curran, 1990; Schrøder, 1987), especially in the combination of quantitative and qualitative methods, but large differences of underlying philosophy and conceptualization remain between the alternative schools. These differences have implications for the goals of research and for the choice of methods.

Issues Arising

This brief review of alternative research approaches helps to identify the main issues and problems that have shaped thinking and research about mass media audiences, aside from the obvious practical need to have basic information. The issues range from the industry-practical and the social-problematic to the purely theoretical, although practice and theory are always connected. As we will see, the transformation of a straight question about the audience into an "issue" or a social problem normally requires the injection of some value judgments, as described in the following paragraphs.

Media Use as a Social Problem

Media policy has often been driven by normative assumptions about the mass audience and a good deal of noncommercial research has been guided

TABLE 2.1 Three Audience Research Traditions Compared

	Structural	*Behavioral*	*Cultural*
Main Aims:	Describe composition; enumerate; relate to society.	Explain & predict choices, reactions, effects.	Understand meaning of content received and of use in context.
Main Data:	Social-demographic, media and time use.	Motives. Acts of choice. Reactions.	Perceptions of meaning. Re social & cultural context.
Main Methods:	Survey & statistical analysis.	Survey; experiment; mental measurement.	Ethnographic; Qualitative.

by the notion that media use may in itself be problematic for society as well as for the individual concerned. "Excessive" media use has been viewed as harmful and unhealthy (especially for children), leading to addiction, dissociation from reality, reduced social contacts, and diversion from education. Television has been the most usual suspect, but before television, films and comics were regarded similarly, while video games and computers have become the latest perpetrators. This pessimistic view is often disputed, and the issue can also be posed positively, in terms of the need to attract audiences to media content that is educative, culturally enriching, or pro-social in its influence. Whatever else, it seems that audience membership readily lends itself to moral and social assessment, and the audience itself is aware of a social norm that condemns undue time spent on media.

The Mass Audience and Social Atomization

The oldest as well as the most general theoretical question about the audience is whether or not it should be treated as a social group (or a public, in the sense outlined earlier) or simply as a mass of isolated individuals. To qualify as the former, an audience would need to show conditions of having boundaries, self-awareness, internal interaction, systems of normative control (Ennis, 1961). The more an audience is viewed as an aggregate of isolated individuals (or a market of consumers), the more it can be considered as a mass. Many subsidiary questions flow from this, including the issue of whether new interactive media possibilities can help to restore group-like collective features to audience experience.

As noted already, there are always alternative ways of regarding the same audience phenomenon and often there are vested interests in such choices. The industry clients of most applied media research and the typical methods of large-scale sample surveys have a bias toward conceiving the audience in terms of aggregate individual behaviors. Survey methods inevitably decompose groups and social networks and can only produce information about aggregates of individuals. This reinforces the tendency to think of "audience behavior" as the outcome of acts of individual consumption rather than as social actions in the Weberian sense of "behavior which is oriented to others" (Freidson, 1953). The group character of audience is ignored or lost sight of as a result.

Audience Behavior
as Active or Passive?

Another broad theoretical issue concerns the degree of "activity" or "passivity" that can be attributed to the audience. By definition, the audience as a mass is passive, because it is incapable of collective action, whereas any true social group has the means and may have the inclination to be active in the sense of choosing a shared goal and participating in its pursuit. Individual acts of media choice, attention, and response can also be more or less active, in terms of degree of motivation, attention, involvement, pleasure, critical or creative response, connection with the rest of life, and so forth. There has always been a tendency, whether explicitly or not, to view active media use as "better" than passive spectatorship.

It is usually supposed that the more active the audience in the senses mentioned, the more resilient and resistant it will be to persuasion, influence, or manipulation, which is also generally viewed as good, although advertisers and propagandists may have other ideas. In principle, active audiences provide more feedback for media communicators, and the relationship between senders and receivers is more interactive. Newer media technologies are thought to have a greater potential for interactivity.

There are new possibilities for audience definition and new types of audience are emerging. Instead of an audience as the attentive mass or group we can, for instance, increasingly speak of a "taste culture" or a "lifestyle" to describe patterns of choice. The more that individuals are free and able to compose their own media "diets" as a result of new technology, the more such types of audience will emerge, having no clear definition in terms of social categories, but held together, nevertheless, by a convergence of cultural tastes, interests, or information needs.

Audiences are now smaller, more numerous, and much less likely to have a fixed and predictable membership. The media have increasing difficulty in identifying and retaining "their" particular audience. Patterns of media use will simply be a part of varied and changing lifestyles. The issue of whether an audience is a group or not might seem to have become increasingly irrelevant. However, it has acquired new currency as a result of new interactive media that seem to have a potential for creating new kinds of "virtual communities."

Alternative Perceptions of the Audience

At one extreme, we find a view of the audience as either a consumer market or a commodity to be sold to advertisers, at so much per thousand. What counts are numbers and purchasing power. Alternatively, the audience can be approached in normative and relational terms, with a genuine communicative purpose. What matters then is its composition, its engagement with communicators and content, the quality of attention and response, its loyalty, commitment, and continuity.

Also at issue here is the dilemma referred to above, between research for control or for liberation and protection of the audience. Whose side is the researcher on? This question has become inextricably mixed up with the question of methods and the built-in bias of different research approaches. The history of research into audiences has been troubled by a fundamental conflict of view between practitioners of quantitative, survey, or experimental research and advocates of alternative, more qualitative, and intensive research. The former seems more inclined to serve the goals of management, the latter claims to take the point of view, and to "be on the side," of the audience.

The qualitative option, which is often claimed as more critical of the media and more sympathetic to the audience, requires close attention to the details of the context of reception and use and also to the meanings that may be derived from content received. It also involves a resistance to the head-counting of commercial audience research for control and management.

Implications of New
Media Technology

Finally, there is the question of the future of media, especially as a result of the changes in communication technology described above, which have led to opposing predictions and valuations. One proposition is that audiences will become more and more fragmented and will lose their national, local, or cultural identity. There will also be an increasing gap between the media rich and the media poor. Another negative view of new electronic media is that they strengthen the potential for social control and surveillance (Gandy, 1989; Spears & Lea, 1994). On the other hand, new kinds of integration may compensate for the loss of older forms, more options for audience formation are available to more people, and there could be more freedom and diversity of communication and reception.

The critical theorist Enzensberger (1972) was one of the first to envisage a radical transformation as a result of new communication technologies, undermining the old state and capitalistic monopolies. New types of community could also emerge, based on interactive communication, untrammelled by cultural barriers. These predictions remain largely in the realm of speculation. The search for answers depends not only on collecting evidence but also on the value perspective adopted. Do we, for instance, prefer the collective virtues of old mass media audiences or the cultural mobility and freedom from social ties of the electronic highway?

Conclusion

As long as the media continue to grow and to matter to society, we can expect audience theory and research to flourish. This review of issues suggests that there are some perennial concerns, although there are also some shifts, reflecting changing technology and changing social values and conditions.

THREE

Typologies of Audience

The Duality of the Audience

The history of mass media indicates that audiences can originate both in society and in media and their contents. People stimulate an appropriate supply, or the media attract people to what they choose to offer. If we take the first view, we can consider media as responding to the general needs of a national society, local community, or preexisting social group. They also respond to the specific preferences actively expressed by particular sets of individuals—for instance, the politically active, or business people, or youth, or followers of sport, and so on. Alternatively, if we consider audiences as primarily created by the media, we can see that they are often brought into being by some new technology (as with the invention of film, radio, or television) or they are attracted by some additional "channel," such as a new magazine or radio station.

We can speak of the "television audience" or the "film-going public" as well as of the readership for a particular newspaper or the loyal viewers of a favorite television station. Audiences are also formed as a result of some new format or type of content, some performer, or a compelling presentation

25

(possibly of limited duration), perhaps backed by intensive marketing and publicity. The media are continuously seeking to develop and hold new audiences for content genres, authors, performers, particular products (e.g., films, books, or "shows"). In doing so they may anticipate what might otherwise be a spontaneous demand or they may identify potential needs and interests that have not yet surfaced. This is certainly what modern media managers try to do.

In the continual flux of media audience formation and change, the sharp distinction made at the outset is not easy to perceive or to demonstrate. Over time, media provision to preexisting social groups and media recruitment of social categories to the content offered have become hard to distinguish from each other. Media-created needs have also become indistinguishable from "spontaneous" needs, or both have fused inextricably. Nevertheless, the theoretical distinction between receiver- and sender-created demand is a useful one for mapping out different versions of audience that have been introduced. The distinction is set out in Figure 3.1, first between society and media-created needs and, second, between the different levels at which the process operates, whether at macro- or micro level. The four main types that are identified in Figure 3.1 are further described and explored in the following sections of this chapter.

The Audience as
Group or Public

An audience as a group or public is a collectivity that has an independent existence prior to its identification as an audience. The clearest examples are now likely to be either historical or small scale, since it is increasingly hard for the group-like conditions of interactivity, normative regulation, and "bound-edness" to be met in a modern society, let alone for them to define an audience. However, publications set up by political or religious bodies or other associations to serve the purposes of their own organization and members still meet the criteria. Party and church newspapers were (and sometimes still are) intended to facilitate internal communication and to support external activities (such as recruiting new members or spreading the word). They normally provide a means of linking leaders to their grass roots, increasing cohesion, and signaling the identity of the group.

		SOURCE	
		SOCIETY	MEDIA
LEVEL	MACRO	i. Social group or public	iii. Medium or channel audience
	MICRO	ii. Gratification set	iv. Audience for particular media content

Figure 3.1. A Typology of Mass Media Audience Formation

There have been many variants of this type of audience. In the case of the press, a "strong" version is exemplified by Lenin's notion of the "vanguard" press (e.g., the social revolutionary journal *Iskra*) whose aim was organization and propaganda carried out by a revolutionary elite (Hopkins, 1970). Later on, Communist Party publications were not really meant for the masses but for the in-group of party members. At the other end of the spectrum, we might think of some present-day newspapers that are largely nonideological and commercial, but that still retain a loose affiliation to a political party or ideology. Editorial support is given at elections, but there is otherwise little influence from politics on the general content of the newspaper.

Under today's conditions, the best example of a media audience that is also in some sense a social group is probably the readership of a local newspaper or the listener group of a community radio station. Here the audience shares at least one significant social/cultural identifying characteristic—that of shared space and membership of a residential community. Local media can contribute significantly to local awareness and sense of belonging (Janowitz, 1952; McLeod et al., 1996; Rothenbuhler, Mullen, De Carell, & Ryan, 1996; Stamm, 1985). Local residence defines and maintains a wide range of media-relevant interests (e.g., leisure, environmental, work-related, social networks, etc.). Local media advertising serves local trade and labor markets. Social and economic forces together reinforce the integrative role of local media. Even if a local medium goes out of business, the local community that forms its audience will persist.

The group character of local media audiences may, even so, be quite weak since a shared space often conceals a great disparity of other population attributes, depending on the kind of locality. Some local areas are just residential locations without any institutional bonds or common identity, little more than a number of people who share the same shopping facilities but who otherwise live private lives and have a high degree of geographical mobility. It is unlikely that media on their own can ever be a substitute for an otherwise missing sense of identification. In addition, local media rarely have exclusive audiences, but often form just the lowest level in a hierarchy of national and metropolitan media provision. Concentration of ownership and of editorial organization have often diminished the genuinely local character of newspapers. Networking of content and ownership has often done the same for local radio.

Beyond the case of local media, there are other circumstances where shared characteristics, relative homogeneity, and stability of composition indicate the existence of some independent and group-like qualities in the audience. Newspapers are often characterized by readerships of varying political leaning, reflecting continuing political diversity in democratic societies. Readers express their political identity by their choice of paper as well as finding reinforcement for their beliefs. Newspapers and magazines may respond by shaping their contents and expressing opinions accordingly.

However, the widespread trend toward more neutral (or "objective") news and the competition for circulation (plus press concentration) have reduced whatever degree of political profiling and audience identification that still remains. Newspapers try to capture larger and thus more heterogeneous groups, and clear political identification of newspapers is often just a sign of a declining or aging readership.

What it means for an audience to be a social group can also be appreciated by considering the extreme reverse case—that of the mass or total audience. At one stage of their development, for instance, many national television broadcasting services consisted of very few channels (or even one) that had to serve an entire national population. The audience consisted of everyone, and broadcasters were constrained to avoid political or other bias. They could not easily appeal differentially to social groups within the total audience.

Nevertheless, the early television audience, despite its size and heterogeneity, could possibly have qualified as a certain kind of public in the sense meant here, since it was distinctively *national* and content provision was also national. The globalization of content has reduced the homogeneity of experience in this sense. More relevant today is the large and heterogeneous audience sought by commercial broadcasting channels offering something for everyone.

Public service broadcasting, where it exists, also attracts an audience with some of the features of a genuine public. The service is itself normally accountable to the general public through a variety of institutional means, including the system of finance (usually a compulsory license fee for all households) and by the political system. It also has an obligation to serve distinct minority audiences. A similar situation arises, in principle at least, in respect to public television (PBS) in the United States, where viewer/listener donations are supposed to forge a bond between media and audience (Avery, 1993).

An often cited example of an audience as a public or social group is found in Holland. Broadcasting is provided by several independent voluntary, non-commercial associations with their own distinctive political, religious, or cultural leaning and that recruit their own members among the national (license-paying) public. Audience attachment to a chosen organization is often signaled and cemented by subscribing to the association's TV program guide. Although the system has been gradually emptied of its original meaning, under pressures of commercial competition and social change (Ang, 1991), it still survives, and it embodies a unique form of relationship between media and television (Avery, 1993). The system serves as a reminder that under certain conditions of social and media structure audiences can still be like-minded social groups, although experience has also shown how vulnerable such a system is to changes in the wider cultural and social environment and to the impact of market forces. The trend of change is clearly against this model of audience formation.

These examples are in contrast to the case of a commercial system, where audience members are customers or consumers and the rules of the market prevail, including that of "buyer beware." Nevertheless, media professionalism can still lead mass communicators to treat their audience as if it were an autonomous group or an active public to which they have specific responsibilities, for instance by full and fair reporting of politics.

There are other examples of audience groups and special publics. For example, the broad term "alternative" media (Downing, 1984) embraces a wide range of more or less oppositional media channels that can be considered to carry on the tradition of the early radical and party press, especially in developing countries. Many such media are "micro-media," operating at a grassroots level, discontinuous, nonprofessional, sometimes persecuted or just illegal. The *samizdat* publications—forbidden under communism, the opposition press in Pinochet's Chile, or the underground press of occupied Europe during World War II are well-known examples. The publics for such media are often small, but they are likely to be intensely committed. They usually have clear social and political goals.

The development of local cable and local radio has had a potential to increase the number of separate channels and thus of minority voices (and thus listener groups), whether legally or not (Jankowski, Prehn, & Stappers, 1992; Kleinsteuber & Sonnenberg, 1990). This development has been especially helpful in the case of groups with a clear and strong identity and a wish to have their own media. Many ethnic and linguistic minorities, often immigrant in origin, have benefited. Minority media of this kind are enduring and significant, although they may not seem to weigh heavily against the big battalions of the major media. They are also dependent on favorable economic and social conditions.

A more familiar type of audience that fits the social group criteria named relates to publications (it usually has been print media) that serve or support professional and social identifications, often circulating within a particular, though widely dispersed, network. Here, the audience shares certain goals, interests, or understandings; sometimes it forms around a particular public issue. At some point, a notional line divides those "audiences" that are in the public sphere from those in private, expert, or professional circles. Dedicated in-house publications for the personnel of an organization, or professional and scientific journals, clearly belong to the latter category, and publications for supporters of social causes like Greenpeace or Amnesty International belong in the former. New media technologies have helped in the growth of such audiences, since reproduction and distribution are easier and cheaper. The Internet and the Web are the latest in the line of technologies that retain and reclaim the channels of communication for the small group or the very dispersed public.

The Gratification Set
as Audience

The term *gratification set* is chosen to refer to multiple possibilities for audiences to form and re-form on the basis of some media-related interest, need, or preference. The use of the word *set* implies that such audiences are typically aggregates of dispersed individuals, without mutual ties. While the audience as "public" often has a wide range of media needs and interests and derives its unity from shared social characteristics, the gratification set is identified by a particular need or type of need (which may, nevertheless, derive from social experience). To a certain degree, this type of audience has gradually supplanted the older kind of public, the result of differentiation of media production and supply to meet distinctive consumer demands. Instead of each public (whether based on place, social class, religion, or party) having its own dedicated medium, many self-perceived needs have stimulated their own corresponding supply.

The phenomenon is not new, because early popular newspapers, as well as gossip, fashion, and "family" magazines, have long catered to a diverse range of specific but overlapping audience interests. The needs served by these publications were mainly for practical information, diversion, and gossip, which also lubricated everyday social life. In the present period, the decline of religious and political commitment and the increased commercialization of media have accelerated the growth of this kind of media.

Over time, a much wider range of interests has been provided for, with each type of medium (film, book, magazine, radio, phonograph records/CDs, etc.) packaging its potential audience appeal in a variety of ways. Such categories are usually based on a mixture of sociocultural and content criteria. People from a particular educational or occupational milieu, for instance, are assumed to have a certain kind of taste, and the same applies to age and gender differences. Combinations of social characteristics are also used to identify a particular lifestyle that also includes a component of media preference (see Chapter 6, under "Lifestyle"). The sets of readers/viewers/listeners that result from a highly differentiated and "customized" supply are unlikely to have any sense of collective identity, despite some shared social-demographic characteristics.

Relevant here is the concept of "taste culture," which was coined by Herbert Gans (1957) to describe something like the audience brought into being by the media, based on a convergence of interests, rather than by shared locality or social background. He defined it as "an aggregate of similar content chosen by the same people" (in Lewis, 1981, p. 204). Taste cultures are less sets of people than sets of similar media products—an outcome of form, style of presentation, and genre that are intended to match the lifestyle of a segment of the audience. The more this happens, the more there is likely to be a distinctive social-demographic profile of a taste culture.

Research in the tradition of "media uses and gratifications" has shed light on the nature of the underlying audience demands and on the way in which they are structured (see Chapters 5 and 6). The motivations expressed for choice of media content and the ways in which this content is interpreted and evaluated by the audience point to the existence of a fairly stable and consistent structure of demand. Social experience plays a part in stimulating requirements from media. For instance, situations of uncertainty can lead to a search in the media for advice or models of behavior; social isolation can lead to media use for companionship or for conformity to peer culture; curiosity about the world and one's place in it promotes attention to media news and information (Blumler, 1985).

The composition of actual audiences as gratification sets is always changing, but causes that underlie the specific (and fleeting) audiences that form for a particular series, film, genre, type of music, and so on are also a product of recurring and predictable forces. The *idea* of an audience as characterized by some particular social or psychological need arising out of experience is significant in the "discourse" about audiences and is helpful in describing audiences. The notion of potential audiences identified according to some social or cultural category is also important to the media industry since it often provides the guidelines for developing new media services and coping with competition.

The Medium Audience

The third version of the audience concept (in Figure 3.1) is the one that identifies it by the choice of a particular type of medium—as in the "television audience" or the "cinema-going public." The earliest such usage has already been mentioned: the "reading public"—the small minority who could and did read books, when literacy was not very common. The reference is usually to those whose behavior or self-perception identifies them as regular and attracted "users" of the medium concerned, although it can be expanded to become a rather loose reference to all reached by a medium.

Each medium—newspaper, magazine, cinema, radio, television, phonograph record/CD—has had to establish a new set of consumers or devotees and the process continues, with the diffusion of "new media," such as the Internet or multimedia. It is not especially problematic to locate relevant sets of people in this way, but the further characterization of these audiences is often crude and imprecise, based on broad social-demographic categories.

This type of audience is close to the idea of a "mass audience" as described in Chapter 1 under "The Audience as Mass," since it is often very large, dispersed, and heterogeneous, with no internal organization or structure. It also corresponds to the general notion of a "market" for a particular kind of consumer service. By now most such audiences are so overlapping that there is little differentiation involved, except in terms of subjective affinity and relative frequency or intensity of use. The audience for any one mass medium is often identical with the audience for another.

Even so, this version of the audience concept retains some relevance, as media forms change and succeed one another. Being a "member" of the audience for film, for instance, involves learning some elements of a role, certain habits as well as particular understandings and perceptions of a medium and its genres. These are things that develop in social interaction in a particular cultural setting. The full meaning of a particular medium audience varies from place to place and time to time.

For example, in the 1940s, before television, the film audience was identical with the cinema-going audience—numerous, youthful, and gregarious, accustomed to large, smoke-filled auditoria, organ music, patiently queuing in the rain, totally dependent for a supply of content on a remote and slow-moving production and distribution business. The film audience of today no longer coincides with the cinema-going audience. It is more home-bound and diverse, older than the cinema audience, accustomed to endless choice from the film archives of the past and stocks of the present, little troubled by censors, hardly limited by cost, supplied by home video and television. There is no longer such a thing as a "film fan," though there are "cult films," which can now have a larger following than in the days of dependence on cinema exhibition.

There is evidence that the audience continues to differentiate among media, according to their particular social uses and functions (Kippax & Murray, 1980) or according to their perceived advantages and disadvantages. Media have fairly distinctive images (Perse & Courtright, 1993). Research has shown that some media are substitutable for each other for certain purposes, while others have distinctive uses (Katz, Gurevitch, & Haas, 1973). Competition among different media for audience and advertising income is intense and these differences play a part. The "medium audience" is an important concept for those who want to use the media for purposes of advertising and other campaigns, despite the lack of exclusivity. A key decision in advertising is often that concerning the "media-mix," the division of an advertising budget among the alternatives, taking into account the characteristics of each medium, the audience it reaches, and the conditions of reception.

In media economics, the issue of media *substitutability* continues to be important and often turns on the extent to which distinctive medium audiences persist (Picard, 1989). Several considerations come into play, aside from the questions of audience size and demographics. Some messages are best delivered in a domestic or family context, indicating a choice of television, while others may be individual and more risqué, indicating posters or magazines. Some may be appropriate in an informational context, others against a background of relaxation and entertainment. From this perspective, the audience for a medium is chosen not only on the basis of socioeconomic characteristics, but with reference to typical content carried and the sociocultural associations and context of the media behaviors concerned.

Audiences Defined by Channel or Content

The identification of an audience as the readers, viewers, listeners of a *particular* book, author, film, newspaper title, or television program seems much less problematic. It is the usage with which audience research in the "bookkeeping" tradition is most comfortable, and it seems to pose few problems of empirical measurement. There are no hidden dimensions of group relations or consciousness to take account of, no psychological variables of motivation that need to be measured. It is the audience in this very concrete sense on which the business of the media turns most of all. For this reason, specific content or channel has usually been privileged as a basis for defining audiences, especially in industry-related research.

This version of audience is also consistent with market thinking, according to which audiences are sets of consumers for particular media products. The audience consists either of paying customers or the heads and pockets delivered to advertisers per unit of media product and charged for accordingly. It is expressed as the "ratings," the "numbers" that are central to the media business. They provide the main criterion of success in any game of media politics, even where profit is not involved. Increasingly, it is the dominant meaning of the term *audience,* the only one with immediate practical significance and clear market value. It also involves a view of the audience as a *product* of the media—the first and indubitable *effect* of any medium.

Despite the seeming lack of ambiguity, there is more to be said on the subject and some hidden complications. The latter arise first from the fact that there are alternative definitions of the "physical" audience thus indicated. The complete audience can never be measured in practice, only reconstructed or estimated after the event. The audience for a particular newspaper title, for instance, can be defined alternatively in terms of subscribers, or households reached, or readers. There are normally wide variations in the degree of reading within the latter group. Audiences for radio and television programs are also made up of individuals giving widely varying degrees of time or attention.

There are also big variations in the degree to which the contents in question are actually chosen or preferred by their audiences, since actual choices are often made by others. It turns out that this version of the audience concept is hardly less of an abstraction than any other. It only works if we arbitrarily define audience in terms of time/space—the time estimated as given by a set of individuals to a "transmission," or a time-/place-located publication. The great advantage, nevertheless, is the fact that it can be quantified and once this has been done, the rules of mathematics are ultimately unassailable.

This sense of audience is a valid one, but we cannot be limited to it. There are, for instance, audiences in the sense of "followers" or fans of television or radio serials and series, which cannot be unambiguously measured. There is no certain way of deciding on the relative value of the extent or the depth of media usage or how to draw the line between devoted and casual spectators. There are audiences for genres and types of content of innumerable kinds that can be defined in terms of spending time or money or expressing preferences, although the boundaries of such content categories are often unclear. There are also audiences for particular films, books, and songs and also for stars, writers, and performers that only accumulate over time to a significant number or proportionate reach. All of these are relevant aspects of the audience experience, though they usually evade any but the most approximate measurement.

This brings us again to the yet more complex question of fans and fandom, which has already been raised. It would seem that the term refers to any set of extremely devoted followers of a media star or performer, performance, or text (L. Lewis, 1992). They are usually identified by great, even obsessive attachment to their object of attraction. Often they show a strong sense of awareness and fellow-feeling with other fans. Being a fan also involves a pattern of supplementary behavior, in dress, speech, other media use, consumption, and more.

Fandom is often associated in the view of critics with immaturity and mindlessness, an outcome of mass culture and an example of mass behavior. The results sometimes seem bizarre from a conventional point of view (e.g., the adulation of dead stars like Elvis Presley), but they underline the potential for media experience to form the basis of distinctive subcultures and identifications. Not only are fans often organized social groups, but they interact very actively with their object of attention and affection. Moreover, fandom is a very old phenomenon and not at all confined to so-called mass culture. The worlds of sports, opera, ballet, theater, and literature have long exemplified essentially the same phenomenon.

The rise of fandom has been interpreted critically as evidence of manipulation and exploitation—something encouraged by the media to strengthen ties with products and performers, to help with publicity, and in order to make extra money from merchandising and other media spin-offs. It helps in extending the life of products and to maximize profit. While this is true, there is an alternative perspective, according to which fandom shows not manipulation by the media but the "productive power" of audiences (Fiske, 1992). According to this view, the fans actively create new meaning out of the materials offered, building up systems of cultural discrimination, stylistic display, social identification, and association that serve to detach the fan group from the manipulative grip of the media.

Whether one treats fan groups as social groups or artificial creations of media industries, they certainly add another complication to the audience view under discussion. Audiences made up of fans are not simply passive targets for marketing strategies of the media. In any actual audience (depending on the content) there will probably be some fans, and some media content will lead to the development of a fan group while others will not. This matters a great deal to the media, especially with respect to music, books, and films. The development of fandom is unpredictable and often unexpected. It is hard to explain, for example, why some television shows and films develop a cult following or prove able to recruit audiences continually in other times and places.

The Breakup of the Mass Audience:
New Types Emerge

The variants of the audience typology discussed above all share one thing in common: They relate mainly to circumstances of *mass communication*—center-peripheral forms of communication flow in which "receivers" are separated from and unknown to "senders." Production, distribution, and consumption are separated. Historically, the development of "the audience" began with the crowd gathered in one spot to view or listen. It gradually became larger in scale, more dispersed, and yet more impersonal. The ultimate mass media audience is a vast aggregate that attends to the same message at the same time. It is clear, even so, that there are many variants of audience, and audience-sender relations to be found in what we call "mass communication." The large-scale, anonymous, mass variant of sender-media relations is not the only possibility, and many actual media audiences are both small in scale and cemented by social and affective ties to communication sources.

Media audiences are often typified according to the social relations that they exhibit (e.g., whether they are detached, distant, unbalanced, etc.) or the degree of social group characteristics (e.g., whether cohesive, bounded, enduring, etc.). Even under conditions of mass communication, we can envisage audiences as varying considerably in these terms, as can be seen from the discussion above of the audience as public or social group. This issue is raised if we look at audiences from a sociological perspective, but there are other reasons for considering the relationships involved in *media use behavior*. New interactive communication technology, in particular, invites attention to the topic.

Bordewijk and van Kaam (1986) have identified the key variables that differentiate information systems first in terms of the centrality or otherwise of the store of information and, second, in terms of control over access—in effect over who (sender or receiver) chooses the subject matter to be received/consulted and over the point in time at which this takes place. The approach assumes a set of participants arranged in the pattern of a wheel, with a rim around a central hub. Communication flows can occur directly among any of the participants at the rim or between the center and any one or more of the peripheral participants. By considering each participant (including the center) as having a store of information that is drawn on, or added to, in communication, a fuller picture of the possible patterns can be arrived at. By cross-tabulating "information store" against "control over choice of time and subject," in terms of whether one is "centrally" or "individually" located, four categories of relationship can be arrived at. The resulting typology is set out in Figure 3.2.

Each type of relation also implies a type of audience. The *allocutive audience* (e.g., concert, lecture, television, book, etc.) stands for the traditional mass media audience in a situation of one-directional communication. The term *allocution* itself is derived from the Latin word for the address by a Roman commander to an assembled body of troops. Such an audience can be of many types, but it is always in some degree dependent on the source (or medium) for decisions about publication frequency and content. The "closer" the audience is, socially or physically, to the source (as in the case of media with especially active publics or whose members form a group), the more autonomous it can be considered. The allocutory type is accentuated in the large, dispersed audience for popular media, such as national network television or the mass press. It is characterized by limited possibilities for "feedback" and communication flow is essentially one-way.

The *consultation* type of audience arises where individuals can choose when and what to attend to from the supply or store available from a central source. This involves an extension of the typical mass media situation. While some audiences for some mass media (e.g., newspapers) can behave in a consultatory mode—for example by selecting content according to interest and convenience—a genuinely consultatory audience exists only for those media that are designed to maximize the power of choice by the user. Typical are computer-based systems such as the Internet, CD-ROM, video-on-demand, or on-line newspapers, while broadcast teletext is designed with the same type of audience behavior in mind. The idea is not new, although the technology for fully realizing it is. Other media, such as videos and even books and phonograph records/CDs, wherever "library" facilities exist, imply a similar definition of the audience as active searcher.

In general, consultation as a form of media use liberates the individual from the constraints of belonging to an audience as defined by the media source, and also decomposes the audience in the older, allocutive, sense. Such "audiences" are individualized sets of information consumers, although they may still be patterned by social factors. If each individual composes a personal "menu" of information, there is no shared audience experience in terms of content, although the concept of a "medium audience" remains.

While the *conversation* pattern, in which control is individual on both sides, also seems to undermine the audience in the accepted sense, it does

		Control of Information Store	
		Central	Individual
Control of time and subject	Central	**ALLOCUTION**	REGISTRATION
	Individual	**CONSULTATION**	CONVERSATION

Figure 3.2. Four Patterns of Communication Relationship
SOURCE: Bordewijk and van Kaam, 1986.

identify a situation in which a set of individuals can be connected with each other actively exchanging, sharing, and interacting in a communication relationship. This is made possible by computer-based interactive systems and restores the notion of an active audience, even in an enhanced form. A new kind of audience becomes possible, in which sender and receiver roles are not distinguished. At the very least, the presence of interactive facilities changes the situation of allocution, opening up possibilities for involvement and feedback on a large scale, which were previously unknown in the typical mass medium audience situation.

The growing body of subscribers to the Internet and multimedia can also be considered in this light, as can the set of individuals who make regular use of such facilities as telephone chat-lines and other audiotext facilities. These are not really audiences, but they are sets of media users.

The final entry, *registration,* seems at first sight less relevant to this discussion of audience concepts. It refers to a situation in which an interconnected set of individual network users of a communication facility (for any purpose of their own, whether allocutory, exchange, or consultation) can be kept under observation by and from a center. Either the fact of use or the content used can be placed under surveillance and recorded. This occurs, for instance, for the central billing of telephone calls or Internet usage, even if access to the central register for content is denied on grounds of privacy. The use of "people meters" in audience research is another example of the registration possibility being applied, normally with the knowledge and consent of the users.

The registration pattern is increasingly used and always implies possibilities for control. Its immediate relevance to the extension of the range of audience concepts is limited, although the electronic media audience is necessarily more open to control or intrusion. We may also refer to the concept of a "registered audience," where private communication behavior is recorded and objectified. This last pattern is the one most associated with fears of greater surveillance and control (Gandy, 1989; Spears & Lea, 1994).

This typology opens up a different way of looking at audiences and poses new issues. As noted, it bypasses the question of the group character of sets of media users, although this may still be relevant. Early experiments in interactive local community cable were based on the view that preexisting social relations would stimulate adoption of the new interactive media and vice versa (Dutton, Blumler, & Kramer, 1987). The Internet seems to have given rise to a new kind of community formation based on shared interests among otherwise anonymous interlocutors (Rheingold, 1994). Earlier typologizing was also based on the assumption that audience behavior was essentially public in character, since mass media were by definition operating in the public sphere of society. This assumption, in turn, implies that there is a fairly clear line separating mass communication and interpersonal communication (which is always private).

Both assumptions are called into question by recent developments and by the newer pattern of relations between senders and receivers. For instance, consultative media use takes place for a mixture of private (e.g., planning a journey) and public (e.g., forming an opinion on a public issue) purposes. "Conversational" patterns cover a wide range of applications, public as well as private, as growing experience with the Internet demonstrates. Registration has the potential for making private audiences and private exchange into publicly accessible data.

Alternative Models of the
Audience-Sender Relationship

There is at least one other path toward a typification of the audience and of audience experience that deserves notice. This also depends on the relationship between source and receiver and derives from a mutual differentiation of attitude and purpose. It can best be explained in terms of three alternative models of the communicative relationship, one described as a *transmission* model, another as an *expressive* or *ritual* model, and a third as an *attention* model (McQuail, 1994).

The three modes of audience orientation and related experiences can be approximately summed up by the terms: *cognitive processing; sharing and normative commitment;* and *attention giving.* They are not mutually exclusive or incompatible, nor do they necessarily help to distinguish among media, channels, or specific types of content. Nevertheless, there are likely to be some systematic and general differences among audiences according to this distinction.

Audience as Target

In the transmission model, the communication process is considered primarily as the sending of signals or messages over time for the purposes of control or influence. The receiver, and thus the audience, is perceived as a *destination* or *target* for the purposeful transfer of meaning. This model applies, for example, to education and many kinds of public information campaigns, as well as some kinds of advertising. It can apply equally to instrumental uses as defined by the audience, for instance many "consultative" uses of media as outlined above.

Audience as Participants

According to the ritual or expressive model (Carey, 1975), communication is defined in terms of sharing and participation, increasing the commonality between sender and receiver, rather than in changing "receivers" in line with the purpose of the "sender." In Carey's view, this kind of communication is "not directed towards the extension of messages in space [over distance] but the maintenance of society in time; not the act of imparting information, but the representation of shared beliefs" (p. 10). Communication is not instrumental or utilitarian, and the attitude of the audience is likely to be playful or personally or morally committed in one way or another. Audience members are essentially participants.

Audience as Spectators

The third audience type arises in a model of communication in which the source does not seek to transmit information or beliefs, but simply to capture the attention of an audience, regardless of communicative effect. Audience attention is what is measured by ratings and thus cashable in the form of subscriptions, box office receipts, and payments from advertisers. It is also cashable in terms of status and influence within media and in society generally. Fame and celebrity are more likely to result from sheer amount of public exposure than from measured "effects" or from measures of audience "appreciation." For mass communicators, high ratings (which record attention) offer the least ambiguous and most tradeable form of feedback and reward. Audience attention as "spectatorship" is temporarily but not deeply involving. It implies no "transfer of meaning" or sharing or deepening of ties between sender and receiver (Elliott, 1972). Time spent with a medium is the main criterion of attention, even though it may only represent time-filling or diversion, or just a way of having some privacy.

Conclusion

In this chapter, we have explored different ways of expressing the meaning of the term *audience*. It is clear that there are choices and that these depend on several quite different factors, especially to do with the characteristics of media as carriers, the cultural nature of content, the particular purposes of sending and receiving, and the social circumstances of audience experience. "Audience behavior" can mean very different things, ranging from chance exposure to media to planned and deeply involving encounters. However, there are also fundamentally different ways of *perceiving* audiences, depending on whether we adopt the view of the media industry, that of the society, the self-view of the media public, or the concerns of audience theory.

This aside, it seems that actual audiences, as empirically constituted, can be differentiated according to two main dimensions: one of time duration, another of degree of attachment or engagement. Audiences are sometimes complex and enduring formations, with deep social roots, although much more often they are fleeting and fickle. The subjective significance attached to being in an audience is also extremely variable, depending as it does on circumstances of the moment, personal taste, as well as the type of content concerned.

FOUR

Questions of Media Reach

The Need to Know the "Objective" Audience

The least problematic version of the audience concept is probably that which underlies the "ratings" in their various forms. The questions that then arise stem almost exclusively from what has been called the "institutional" point of view—the view from media industries. According to Ang (1991), "institutional knowledge . . . is [interested] in 'television audience' which it constructs as an objectified category of others to be controlled" (p. 154). It is primarily the media providers and some communicators themselves who need to know just who and how many are reached by their messages. This point of view has largely been taken over by mainstream mass communication research, especially when it is carried out for some purpose of measuring "effect" or investigating some media-linked "social problem." The dominant model of effect research or "planned communication" (Windahl, Signitzer, & Olson, 1992) still calls for precise knowledge of who is targeted and reached by which channels and messages, as a condition for estimating effects and evaluating success.

Media providers need to know a great deal about the extent of media reach (which is at the same time a measure of audience attention) for reasons of finance or policy or for organization and planning. These concerns create a strong vested interest in the "canonical audience" referred to by Biocca (1988a, p. 127). This concept derives from the theater and cinema and refers to a physical body of identifiable and attentive "spectators." A belief in the existence of such an audience is essential to the routine operation of media. As Tunstall (1971) pointed out with respect to newspaper journalism, reaching and pleasing an audience is a "coalition" goal (one on which all can agree) of the diverse and often competing interests within a large media organization (especially management, technical, and editorial staff). The fact of having an audience, and the right one as well, is a necessary condition of media organizational survival, and it has to be continually demonstrated.

This condition of dependence on external information about the audience is relatively new historically. It has become increasingly problematic, and it is also the site of competing claims (e.g., over the penetration and actual use of new technologies like satellite, cable, and multimedia). For early print publications, the only essential data about the audience were the size of print-runs, which determined costs, and the number of copies sold, which determined income. No doubt authors and editors often had a personal interest in how many and what kind of readers were ultimately reached, but such knowledge was only sporadically available. The early film industry could be largely satisfied with box-office returns, supplemented by occasional surveys of the film-going public (Handel, 1950).

Early propagandists and political parties using print media certainly wanted to reach and influence as many people as possible, but the main incentive to learning more about the audience "reached" was the growth of paid commercial advertising in print and outdoor media in the later 19th and early 20th centuries. Several types of knowledge about the audience became relevant, especially concerning: its size; its geographical distribution; and its social composition. Each of these was relevant to advertisers and could affect the price that could be asked for space.

No doubt, such questions were usually settled initially by personal, local, knowledge and rule of thumb. Each succeeding medium has not only introduced some new definition or nuance into the definition of "empirical" audiences, as seen by media institutions, but has given rise to new problems of measurement. Radio and then television broadcasting were especially challenging because audience presence and attention leaves no material trace and there is no independent validation of estimates of reach. The multiplication of new channels and new media has compounded the problem.

Different Media, Different Concepts of Reach

The diversity of audience types has already been discussed, but more needs to be said about how audiences for successive media (most of which still survive and coexist) have been defined. In the case of the *book* medium, there are two main possibilities of definition: those who read books with some regularity (the reading public), and those who buy books (the book market). Some of the latter are not themselves in the reading public and the reading public is not coextensive with the buying public (because of book borrowing, shared household use, etc.). The different categories are neither cumulative nor overlapping and there is rarely much information to be had about any one of them, except for what can be extrapolated from sales and library lending figures. The audience for any particular book title is a less ambiguous entity—consisting of the set of actual readers in a given time frame—but its boundaries are, even so, not self-evident.

The *newspaper* or *periodical* medium offers at least four different measures of audience reach that matter to one or another institutional interest. First, there is the total or potential newspaper/magazine *reading public*. This is open to more than one interpretation, since it can be defined in terms of reading ability, availability to read, or regularity of reading. In some circumstances the reading public comes close to being the whole adult population, but the incidence and regularity of reading seems to have peaked and declined. Second, there is the *paying readership* (those who buy newspapers or magazines). The extent of this may for practical purposes be equated in extent with the number of copies sold, although it cannot be assumed that purchase equals reading. The distinction between the regular paying subscriber and the occasional buyer of single copies is also important to the publisher, although not to the advertiser.

Third, there is the *reading audience* of a particular publication (or title), which is normally a good deal larger than the number of copies sold, since each copy is usually read by more than one person, especially when copies are sold to households/families. This audience is the equivalent of that actually "reached," sometimes called the "cumulative audience" or the total "circulation" of a publication. It is usually measured in terms of the average readership of a single *issue* of the publication in question. This is the audience that matters most to the advertiser. In general, less frequently appearing and more expensive publications (such as glossy magazines) have a higher ratio of reach to sales.

Lastly, there is the *internal audience* for different parts or sections of a given newspaper or magazine. For instance, we can speak of a certain regular audience for sports, or crime fiction, or international news. Normally, this can only be estimated on the basis of a sample survey and can never be measured precisely. As with all media, we can also distinguish in terms of degree of attention and of amount of time spent with reading: The dedicated newspaper reader is different from the casual and short time reader.

The *film* audience, as noted already, has been subject to much diversification. In the early years of the cinema, audience was measured by box-office admissions per film, which could be cumulated over time to give an idea of the total spectators (audience) of any major film. This again is the basic *paying audience.* It is still customary to rank the popularity of films according to the cumulated gross receipts, however little this says about the audience. Admission and other financial data do not indicate the extent and composition of the *film-going public:* the proportion of the population that regularly visits the cinema and its social composition. Only surveys of actual audiences or the general public can provide these data (Handel, 1950; Jowett & Linton, 1980).

There are now at least three other main ways of joining the *paying* audience for film: renting film on video cassettes; buying film cassettes; viewing a film on a cable or satellite subscription movie channel (or via a video-on-demand system). In each case, a single payment can mean several people reached. In addition, there is the very much larger audience for films on "free" television, which is virtually beyond estimation. There is little industry interest in knowing about this audience, beyond what affects balance sheets.

The audience for *music* can also be accounted for in different ways, and there are similarities with film. The main accounting "unit" is the recorded performance that can be personally bought in different forms and accessed by different routes (especially radio and recordings). As with film, there is often a larger global than national market (Burnett, 1990; Negus, 1992). A special feature of the music audience (compared to other media) is the continued significance of the live performance and perhaps also the degree of participation by sections of the audience, either as amateur producers and performers, or by way of dancing and other forms of behavior and expressions of style.

Radio and *television* audiences are conceptually very close, although there are some differences, especially because of circumstances of use. In both cases, there is the *potential* audience consisting of all who own or have access to a receiving set. This audience can be expressed in terms of individuals or households, since the receiving set is sometimes a family or household, rather than an individual, possession. This has long since ceased to apply to radio, and television is moving in the same direction of multiple ownership. Second, there is a *regular* audience of all who use the facility with some regularity (there are even some nonviewers and nonlisteners). Within this regular audience, there are important distinctions according to *degree* of use and subjective *affinity* with the medium.

This leads to the question of listening or viewing as primary or secondary activity, since both can and do accompany other activities, radio more so than television. Conceptually, this is not very crucial, but it matters greatly for measurement (see Twyman, 1994). In addition to these definitions, we need also to recognize the *actual* audience for broadcasting, the one that is present for a particular "program," but that can be accounted for in other ways, such as according to time or type of content. This corresponds to the "internal audience" for the newspaper noted above. Lastly, there is the new and growing audience for recorded television programming and for other (multimedia) uses of the television monitor.

Other less conventional audiences can also be distinguished, for instance for outdoor billboards and video screens, direct mail, audiotext, telephone selling campaigns, and more. There are now almost too many types of media for it to be helpful to discuss in this way. "Old media" change their content and uses of old media also change. The terms and definitions presented here are not fixed. However, the principles of classification remain much the same and we can adapt these to new circumstances.

A Generalized View of Media Reach and Impact

As we have seen, media organizations have always been worried by the "invisibility" of their audiences. This is especially true of radio and television broadcasting where, even with the help of research, the audience size can still only be very indirectly, approximately, and retrospectively estimated. By contrast, music, books, magazines, films, and newspapers all yield some ongoing direct and independent evidence of audience attention and interest.

In the case of broadcasting, not only is the size of the audience unknown, but the quality of reception is extremely unpredictable, with variable attention and much switching between "channels."

Broadcasters are dependent on research (after the event) to know three basic facts about their audience: its size for different channels and programs; the degree of attention given; and the degree of satisfaction or appreciation. Uncertainty has generated much ingenuity in research. The increase in the number of channels as a result of new technology and international transmission has exacerbated the situation, making the "audience" even less predictable, stable, or knowable. On the other hand, some of the new means of delivery (especially by interactive cable) have made precise knowledge of audiences (or receiver set use) possible, even at the moment of use.

The essential features of audience reach, as viewed by the would-be communicator, are presented in Figure 4.1, derived from the work of the Belgian researcher, Roger Clausse (1968). Although this model was developed for the case of broadcasting, it can apply, in principle, to all mass media to cover most of the distinctions made above. The outer band represents the almost unlimited potential for the reception of broadcast messages. In effect it equates audience with a near-universal distribution system. The second band indicates the realistic maximum limits that apply to reception—delineating the *potential* media public, which is defined by residence in geographical areas of reception and by possession of the necessary apparatus to receive, or the means to purchase or borrow publications, phonograph records/CDs, video recordings, and so on. It is also determined by degree of literacy and possession of other necessary skills.

Definitions of availability or eligibility also play a part. For instance, the potential audience might exclude children under a certain age and certain other categories of viewers or listeners (e.g., foreigners or people in institutions). We may also limit the notion of potential audience to those having an affinity with the media concerned as well as habits of use. For some purposes the "potential audience" has also to take account of time of day—distinguishing, for instance, between an early morning, a daytime, and an evening audience.

The third band identifies another level of media public—the *actual* audience reached by a radio or television channel or program or any other medium. This is what is usually measured by sales, admission and subscription figures, reading surveys, and audience ratings (often expressed as a percentage of the potential audience). The fourth and the central bands relate to the *quality* of attention, degree of impact, and potential effect, some of

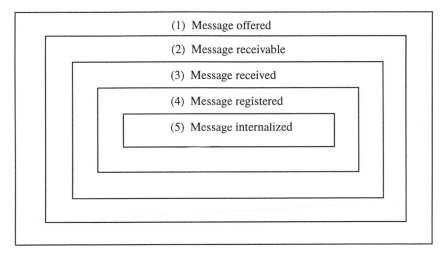

Figure 4.1. A Schema of Differential Audience Reach
SOURCE: Clausse, 1968.

which are empirically measurable. In practice, only a small fragment of the total of *actual* audience behavior can ever be measured, and the rest is extrapolation, estimate, or guesswork.

Clausse commented on the extraordinary degree of instability of audiences and also on the "wastage" represented by this diagram, since most communication receives only a small fraction of its potential attention and impact. He also drew attention to the qualitative differences among media publics, which range from a condition of "communion" where scattered individuals may be brought together by the medium in an intense and shared experience; through one of coherent togetherness; to a mass condition (conglomeration of individuals) represented by the varied, casual, or habitual uses of the media for unplanned diversion.

The question of differential reach and impact of mass media is of more than theoretical interest, since it has to be taken into account in planning communication—especially in campaigns for commercial, political, or informational ends (see Windahl et al., 1992). Most campaigns operate with a notion of a "target group" (of voters, consumers, etc.) that becomes the audience that a campaign tries to reach. This adds another term to our repertoire—that of *target audience,* one with a specified composition in terms of demographic and other attributes.

It is rare for such a target to coincide precisely with the contours of any of the types of audience (or actual audiences) mentioned earlier, but the aim of a campaign source is to maximize the correspondence between the actual audience reached by different media and the target audience as conceived in the campaign plan. The more this is achieved, the more cost-efficient is the campaign (although not necessarily more effective). The target audience is much the same as what has been called in humanistic enquiry the "inscribed" or "implied" audience—that for which an author writes (Sparks & Campbell, 1987). In this tradition, the inscribed audience can be identified from media "texts," which usually contain clues to the tastes, interests, and capabilities of intended recipients, not to mention the stereotypes held by media providers.

While media, such as television, that have very large potential audiences are almost certain to reach all potential target groups in some degree, there is no guarantee that any particular message will reach its goal, or be noticed when it does. The costs of "scattergun" publicity are high and the returns uncertain. For this reason, most campaigners try to use any one medium selectively or a selective combination of different media. The choice is based on estimates of who is likely to be reached and about overlaps between the audiences for different media.

Overlapping Audiences: Different Functions, Places, and Times

It is obvious from what has been said that people normally belong at the same time to several different potential audiences (radio, television, film, etc.) and can even belong to more than one actual audience at the same moment (e.g., listening to the radio while reading). There are several other ways in which audience memberships can be thought of as overlapping. For instance, the audience for one type of content (e.g., news) may be more, or less, coextensive with the audience for another (e.g., sports); people can subscribe to (or read) more than one magazine or newspaper or have an attachment to more than one television channel. All this follows from the diversity of media functions and the ubiquity of media in daily life.

Media also have characteristics that make them suitable for different purposes at different points in a daily or more extended routine. Radio and recorded music are suitable accompaniments for household work or driving;

print media are convenient while sitting down or traveling, especially when alone; cinema is generally a sociable and public medium; and television is still predominantly viewed with others as a means of private, family, or household leisure.

The Spatial Dimension
of Audience Reach

For practical purposes (of advertising, campaigning, designing competitive strategies for ratings or circulation), however, perhaps the most important source of overlap is geographical. There are several criteria for audience differentiation, but *locality* is one of the oldest and most enduring. Boundaries of potential or actual audiences often correspond to a hierarchy of geographical levels: from international, to national, to regional, to metropolitan (or city), to small town and local (or neighborhood). In general, the audience "lower" in the hierarchy is included under the higher-level audience: The reader of a local (or suburban) newspaper can be expected to read a city newspaper and also a national newspaper or magazine (see Picard, 1989, p. 29, for a description of this "umbrella" model of competition). Such publications do not usually compete directly with each other, either in terms of content or for advertising. At the "lowest" level of print media, publications are often free, paid for by advertising. Retail advertising is geographically zoned and national advertising is often different in kind from that in city, local, or regional markets.

This hierarchy of media distribution and audience formation helps as an initial orientation to questions of audience overlap, but the reality is rarely so neat. The situation also varies a great deal from one country to another, depending on geography and media traditions. In the United States, for instance, the daily newspaper is usually that of a city or metropolitan area, with relatively few also reading a "national" newspaper and many individuals making do with a suburban or even a free (local) newspaper. In some European countries (France, Sweden, and Germany, for instance), most daily newspapers are regional rather than national or city papers. Television and radio have not (yet) developed a corresponding hierarchy, but are mainly national in distribution, with the local audience subsumed within the national audience.

For some practical (economic) purposes, what matters is not the absolute size of an audience but the *density of circulation* (or reach) in a given geographical area. A high "density" means that a high proportion of individuals or households in a specific area are reached. This is especially relevant for local advertisers of goods and services. High density of coverage maximizes the cost-efficiency of distribution and advertising. This is the main reason for the viability of "free" newspapers, which have a guaranteed 100% distribution in a given area. It is also the reason for intense competition among newspapers in the same reader (and advertising) market and for the accelerated risk of failure once market share starts to fall below that of a rival.

The same logic drives purely commercial television channels to maximize the size of an audience for a given program, within which certain advertising spots (e.g., for nationally available brand-name products) can expect to reach a high proportion of the general population. In this case, large size also means high density and is therefore cost-efficient. Many target audiences, whether for advertising or information, are not of this kind and require careful choice of appropriate (minority) media.

We can also look at spatial influences in terms of precisely *where* media are actually used in a micro perspective: in which room of a house or outside space (car, train, garden, street, workplace, etc.)? As media multiply and diversify, this micro perspective becomes more important and along with it the need to take account of such factors as gender, lifestyle, social context, and subculture. Questions of audience reach have too often been posed and answered from the point of view of the sender (the administrative view again) rather than that of the receiver.

The Time Dimension
of Audience Reach

The significance of time in the planning of, or accounting for, actual audience reach derives from two features of the situation: the media are produced and distributed on a more or less constant time frequency; and the availability of the audience is mainly a question of the time at people's disposal. Media vary considerably with respect to their time frequency. Books and films appear on an irregular basis and with a long time interval (reflecting a long production process); magazines usually weekly or less often; newspapers weekly, daily, or several editions a day; radio, teletext, and television on a near continuous basis. In theory, media with different appearance cycles do not need to compete with each other directly for the attention of the same audience, although in practice they do compete, since audience availability is also unevenly distributed and time free for media use concentrates at certain points of the day.

There is a significant degree of *cumulation* of audience reach (both of the same and of different media) over any given period, and there are also large variations among media in the amount and pattern of cumulation. For instance, readership of a monthly magazine continues to grow over the whole life of the issue, while a morning newspaper's growth will have peaked within 12 hours. Such patterns are of interest to media industries and are often predictable because of the consistency of the influences on audience formation (see Chapter 5). The main methods for investigation are surveys that retrospectively record different kinds of media use behavior by a given population over a given time period (sometimes in the form of time budgets).

Variable Media Use

The question of the varying *degree* of media use can best be approached from the perspective of the audience itself. At root, differential media reach is the outcome of continuous choices that people make. Even so, for most people media use is a very stable habit as well as being an outcome of numerous specific and motivated behaviors. Some researchers (e.g., Gerbner, Gross, Morgan, Signorielli, & Jackson-Beek, 1979) have argued that the amount of individual "exposure" to television (time spent viewing) is a fundamental and enduring trait, comparable to such demographic characteristics as age and education and with as much influence on attitudes and behavior. The same can be said of some other media behaviors, such as reading a morning or evening newspaper.

People often have an affective attachment to a particular medium that is measurable as a stable attitude and correlated with actual use behavior. Attachment to media is, in general, itself a form of "fandom," which is independent of specific content. Research into the perception of media (Katz et al., 1973; Kippax & Murray, 1980; Perse & Courtright, 1993) shows the differential appeal of media to be associated with certain widely perceived characteristics and uses.

There seems to be a high degree of agreement on what characterizes and differentiates the main media types. The fact that individuals vary a good deal in their affinity for, and propensity to attend to, different media puts the question of media reach in a slightly different light. It calls attention to the fact that media (or channels, or messages) with the highest "ratings" (in the sense of proportion reached) are not necessarily the most effective for every purpose. The relative intensity of attraction has also to be taken into account.

An alternative way of representing reach to that shown in Figure 4.1 would portray a given population as being reached in varying degrees of saturation and frequency. It is not only that some *media* consistently reach more people more often than others, but some *people* are consistently reached more frequently and for longer than others. Those who are hardest to reach can also be much sought-after target groups for would-be communicators. They may have less time to devote to media or are much more selective, with specialized media needs arising out of lifestyle or occupation.

There are some general predictors of variations of this kind. For instance, a preference for audiovisual over print media usually goes with lower education and income, and "heavy" media use usually goes with having more free time at home (housewives, unemployed, elderly, etc.). The more elusive target audience members are quite often also busier and wealthier. Even so, much of the variation in use is the aggregate outcome of individual differences that are not easy to account for in any systematic way.

It is clear from many international comparisons that the frequency and type of media use vary a good deal from one country to another. Even within a fairly similar social and economic environment, such as Western Europe, there are large differences in time spent viewing television (McCain, 1986) and in newspaper reading. The differences seem quite stable over long periods of time. For instance, the average daily amount of time spent viewing television is more than 3 hours in Italy and Britain, but under 2 hours in Holland and Denmark. In general, such findings underline the degree to which audience formation is influenced by the national media structure, social structure, and cultural patterns.

Audience Composition

At an early point in the study of media audiences (see DeFleur, 1970), it became apparent that media use was closely correlated with other social-demographic characteristics—especially age, income, gender, occupation (and combinations of these). Even if audiences were often aggregates made up of scattered individuals, their formation was shaped by forces at work in the social environment that led to distinct patterns in their overall composition. The more choices that became available, the more *selective* people were in their attention, guided by differences of interest or need (Sears & Freedman, 1971; Zillman & Bryant, 1985). These natural tendencies were accentuated by the efforts of media to appeal to different social groups.

As a result, many media show strong and stable patterns in the social profile of their audiences. Sometimes this appears as a rather homogeneous and selected composition, while other media (or particular channels) have socially differentiated audiences. The latter applies, for instance, to many city newspapers, which serve a socially disparate *area* rather than a particular demographic *group*. It also tends to apply to media channels with a near-universal reach, such as national television (by definition, the national audience is heterogeneous), although there is a good deal of social differentiation in the "internal" content choices. Specific tastes and preferences are influenced, of course, by education, age, gender, and other factors.

Audience Diversity: External Versus Internal Forms

The issue of audience *homogeneity* or *heterogeneity* is raised by these remarks and along with it the question of *diversity*. There are normative overtones to each of the three terms, although there is not much consistency about how the norms are applied by critics and social theorists. There are also some paradoxical relations between heterogeneity and homogeneity. The early mass audience was heterogeneous by definition, yet because it was heterogeneous, it could also provide a basis for more democratic communication—all citizens in principle received much the same cultural and informational offerings.

A uniform media diet over time is likely to produce greater cultural homogeneity. From a more critical perspective, however, both the original heterogeneity and the process of homogenization were found undesirable. Heterogeneity implied fragmentation and alienation, while homogenization was disliked because it increased conformity and the potential for manipulation (Marcuse, 1964).

The implicit norm here is that audience formation should most desirably reflect known individual differences (of belief, opinion, taste, background, capacity, etc.). The preferred alternative to the heterogeneous or homogenized mass audience is a multiple array of audiences for different media channels (or types of content), each more or less internally homogeneous in composition according to some relevant characteristic (of politics, religion, cultural taste, locality, etc.). However, this pattern can also be seen as divisive in cultural or political terms—reflecting a stratified, traditional, or even undemocratic society. It follows from these remarks that no fixed normative position is tenable although, generally speaking, diversity has always received a better press than its opposites.

Leaving aside the question of what is most desirable, we can identify two main forms of audience diversity, corresponding more or less to the heterogeneous and homogeneous distinction. One is usually referred to as *internal,* the other as *external* diversity. Internal audience diversity applies where a medium attracts a socially heterogeneous (also often a large) audience and offers a broad range of content to suit the different tastes, interests, and opinions of the available public. General national television channels in many countries fit this description, as do city or local newspapers. Such media typically offer something for everyone, including objective information and a range of opinions, without taking sides.

By contrast, the "external" model assumes a channel or medium with its own editorial line or particular selection of content designed with a particular audience in mind, based on politics, religion, lifestyle, cultural preference, or some other principle. The audience attracted is likely to be homogeneous according to the relevant dimension of content, although the audience for the media system as a whole will be diverse. The political party press, now largely extinct, was the clearest model, although periodicals still often follow this pattern of diversity, following the decline of the general interest magazine (van Zuylen, 1977).

Both the internal and external diversity models can coexist in the same media system, applying differently to different media. The periodical press seems best able to support the external pattern of many separate homogeneous (profiled) audiences, while television and newspapers have largely developed according to the internal pattern. The new technologies that are giving rise to narrowcasting and more "consultative" media use patterns incline to the former. They are suited to offering more specialized television channels (movies, news, sport, art, etc.) as well as diverse information services to suit different needs.

Some current social trends appear independently to encourage the internal model, especially the decline of ideological differences and growing consumerism. Other trends, for instance weaker social control, more social inequalities, and more mobility, may lead to a more differentiated society and a fragmented media system. Most probably it is not a matter of increasing or declining social differentiation, but of a shift in the relative importance of different influences. For instance, lifestyle and taste, and even the mass media themselves, may now be more potent as sources of differentiation than politics and religion. If so, given that media channels are multiplying, we should expect more rather than less audience fragmentation. Somewhat paradoxically, this would imply a growth in the external pattern of diversity.

On Audience Ratings:
Quantity Versus Quality

This chapter has generally presumed that the audience is measurable and can be "accounted" for in the literal sense of being expressed as numbers or proportions, whether actual or estimated. Here and there, however, the notion has surfaced that being in an audience is not only a matter of degree but also of kind. As to degree, there are many possible levels of attention and conscious participation (and also variations in duration and continuity) in audience membership that can only be crudely expressed in ratings (generally percentages of the available or potential audience). As Drew and Weaver (1990) point out, it is often important to distinguish clearly between the *degree of attention* paid and the *frequency of exposure,* especially when questions of potential effect are at issue.

As to quality, there are different dimensions that could be considered. One is the degree of *affinity* with, or *attachment* to, a given medium, irrespective of actual use. Another dimension is expressed in acts of conscious selection of specific contents (e.g., film, books, TV programs) based on the *anticipated satisfaction* from the audience experience. A third might be the degree of *attention* paid, or *involvement* with the media experience, while actually in an audience. Quality can also be equated with high ratings of satisfaction, *appreciation,* or liking, of the kind often asked for in television research. In one way or another, these all reflect degrees of audience *"activity"* (see the section below) that are not normally captured by ratings. There are, of course, many other possible indicators of quality, depending on medium and the specific aims of content.

The quality of audience experience in these terms is not routinely assessed in great detail, although it is not uncommon (in the case of television) to supplement ratings with some measures of audience satisfaction, liking or "appreciation." These are sometimes regarded as more valid and informative than ratings, partly because the latter are often a predictable function of scheduling decisions, determined by timing and the available alternatives. Quality measures can easily vary independently of ratings (especially in the short term), and they are not necessarily very discriminating or easy to interpret (Barwise & Ehrenberg, 1988; Leggatt, 1991). For instance, a television program intended for a minority taste, but seen by a large audience, is likely to receive a low *average* quality rating from its audience. Even if the *intended* audience was very satisfied, the majority of the audience might have inappropriate expectations and be particularly disappointed. However, in general, according to Barwise and Ehrenberg (1988), people watch what they like on television and like what they watch.

Activity and Selectivity

Research into audience selectivity was originally stimulated by hopes or fears about the effects of mass communication. Propagandists and advertisers viewed the large and unselective audience as a suitably receptive target for their persuasive efforts. Critics of mass culture feared that a large and *passive* audience would be exploited and culturally harmed. The media, especially television, were thought to result in increased passivity. There was much concern for children, since passive addiction to one medium after another (comics, films, radio, television) was seen as the enemy of education, discrimination, active recreation, and normal personal and social development (e.g., Himmelweit et al., 1958; Schramm et al., 1961).

It was the would-be media propagandists who were most disappointed by the findings of research, since it soon appeared that selection and avoidance by their target audiences meant that even large-scale media campaigns were most likely to reach the already converted and less likely to reach those they wanted to influence (Hyman & Sheatsley, 1947). The truly passive mass audience proved something of a myth, although television did go some way toward delivering a large audience with relatively low involvement and thus fewer defenses against persuasion (Krugman, 1965).

The solace offered to culture critics and educationists by evidence of limited effects was mixed. Theory fastened on the image of the "obstinate audience" (Bauer, 1964b)—one that might not always be very selective in attention, but was selective in perception and resistant to unwanted influence. At least the audience was not the passive victim portrayed in mass society theory, although controversy remains about how active the typical media audience really is and about what activity means. There is quite a lot of evidence (see, e.g., Kubey, 1986; Kubey & Csikszentmihalyi, 1991) to show that television viewing, at least, is not a very salient activity, nor an object of strong feelings. On the other hand, reading and film-going are likely to be more personally involving.

Biocca (1988b) has reviewed the different meanings and concepts of *audience activity,* proposing five different versions that are to found in the literature, as follows.

1. Selectivity. We can describe an audience as active the more that choice and discrimination are exercised in relation to media and content within media (see Zillman & Bryant, 1985). This is mainly likely to show up in evidence of planning of media use and in consistent patterns of choice. Very heavy media use (especially of television) is likely to be accounted as by definition "unselective" and therefore inactive.

In television research, a distinction has been made between "ritualized" and "instrumental" patterns of use (Rubin, 1984). The former refers to habitual and frequent viewing by people with a strong affinity with the medium. Instrumental use is purposeful and selective, thus more likely to qualify as active. Use of other media, especially radio, music, and newspapers, can be similarly patterned. This version of the activity concept seems to imply that more active users are more sparing with their time. However, very low levels of media use are not necessarily the result of keen discrimination, and it would be eccentric to count media avoidance as, in itself, a sign of "audience activity."

All in all, this is a very weak notion of activity, and selectivity can sometimes just be the response to a large number of media options. Channel switching and "grazing" with a remote control appear to indicate selectivity, although they also imply indecision. Many other kinds of media behavior are by definition "selective": renting videos, buying books and records/CDs, borrowing from a library, and so on, but there may be also be much chance involved.

2. Utilitarianism. Here the audience is the "embodiment of the self-interested consumer." Media consumption represents the satisfaction of some more or less conscious need, such as those postulated in the "uses and gratifications" approach. Active media use here implies rational choice guided by experience and also, if appropriate, some utility expected after the event (e.g., the ability to make a more informed choice). By definition it subsumes "selectivity," although there can be selectivity without utilitarianism.

3. Intentionality. An active audience according to this definition is one that engages in active cognitive processing of incoming information and experience. This type of activity accompanies, rather than precedes, media use although it is often implied by the various forms of subscription to media. Thus, regular subscribers to a publication or media service can be viewed as more active.

4. Resistance to Influence. Following the lines of the "obstinate audience" concept, the activity concept here emphasizes the limits set by members of the audience to unwanted influence or learning. The reader, viewer, or listener remains "in control" and unaffected, except as determined by personal choice. On the other hand, there is also likely to be a correlation between close and regular attention to the media (thus an active attitude and behavior) and a tendency to be influenced. This is likely, for instance, in the case of news (see Robinson & Levy, 1986).

5. Involvement. There are different versions of what this means and how it might be measured, but in general, the more an audience member is "caught up" or "engrossed" in the ongoing media experience the more we can speak of involvement. This can be also called "affective arousal." Although the reference is to a mental state, it can be open to physiological measurement.

Zillman (1980, 1985) has described ways in which arousal and excitement as a result of audiovisual experience can be experimentally stimulated and measured. In general, the more arousal, the stronger the drive to continue the media use behavior. Zillman sees this as especially relevant to explaining the appeal of entertainment and uses of media for "mood control." Involvement may also be indicated by such signs as "talking back" to the television, or even talking about it to fellow viewers while it is on.

These different versions of the audience activity concept do not all relate to the same moment point in the sequence of media exposure. As Levy and Windahl (1985) point out, they may relate to *advance* expectations and choice, or to activity *during* the experience, or to the *postexposure* situation, for instance the transfer of satisfactions gained from the media to personal and social life (e.g., in conversation about media, or based upon media-derived topics).

There are some other aspects of active media use that may be missed by the five variants outlined. For instance, audience activity can take the form of direct response by letter or telephone, whether or not encouraged by the media. Local or community media, whether print or broadcast, may generally have more active audiences, or they have more opportunity to do so. Critical reflection on media experience, whether openly expressed in feedback or not, is another example of audience activity, as is conscious membership of a fan club.

In the case of television, audience appreciation ratings that are either unusually high or low often indicate the presence within a program audience of a set of active viewers who respond very positively or very negatively. The act of recording and replaying from radio or television is another indication of above-average engagement. Finally, we can note the view, examined later in more detail, that audiences often participate in the media experience by giving meaning to it, thus actively *producing* the eventual media "text" (Fiske, 1987, 1992).

The general notion of "audience activity" is evidently an unsatisfactory concept. It is open to diverse definitions, its indicators are very mixed and ambiguous, and it means different things with different media. It is sometimes manifested in behavior, but sometimes it is only a mentalistic construct (an attitude or feeling). According to Biocca (1988b) it is almost empty of meaning in general, because it is *unfalsifiable:* "It is, by definition, nearly impossible for the audience *not* to be active" (p. 77). Despite the inadequacy of activity as a single general concept, there continue to be valid theoretical and practical reasons for retaining it, but only when the chosen version can be clearly defined and empirically tested.

The Transnational Audience

Most media audiences are located within one country, but the reach of media is increasingly extending across national frontiers. This applies especially to film, television, and music. The fact of media transnationalization is not at all new (Tunstall, 1977), but the process is accelerating, especially as a result of new means of distribution and the globalization of media industries and the more universal communicative capacity of music and pictures. The promotion of major international sporting events has also done much to foster the process of media transnationalization (and vice versa).

In theory, such cross-border or global audiences are "lost" to their original communication sources, since they no longer figure in the reckoning of audience size for the original product or distribution channel. In fact, a good deal of internationalized media supply and cross-border flow is planned and monitored. There is an increasing trend for media content to be produced deliberately for the international market, and exports are no longer just a surplus to domestic needs (Wildman, 1994). This applies especially to films, music, television news, and advertising. As a result, we need to distinguish among different kinds of international audience in order to assess the degree and significance of transborder media flow.

Sepstrup (1989, 1990) suggests that three basic forms of international distribution are involved. One type is *multilateral* flow, involving redistribution of content (usually made for home consumption) from one country and production center to many different countries and media destinations for mediated or direct reception in those places. This applies to would-be global TV channels, like MTV, CNN International, BBC World Television, and others, as well as to satellite channels that target audiences in a number of countries. It also applies to the long-standing phenomenon of nationally organized world radio services or channels such as Voice of America, or Radio Moscow. The "audiences" for such media are not easy to keep track of (Mytton & Forrester, 1988), although the control and financing of operations, as noted above, usually requires some feedback about reception, even where transmission has a political or ideological purpose.

The second type overlaps with this and is really *national* redistribution of foreign media products (e.g., foreign films bought for TV or cinema distribution, popular music on radio or recordings, or translations of foreign books). In this case, the selection of foreign content for the audience is made by home-based media channels. There is nothing especially new about this, and the patterns reflect long-standing relations of media dependency, trade, and also cultural affinities. The recruitment of an audience for a "foreign" product will depend on the facts of media culture (e.g., the established appeal of Hollywood films or certain kinds of Western popular music) plus the relevant ties of cultural and linguistic affinity. This is referred to by Hoskins and Mirus (1988; Hoskins, Mirus, & Rozeboom, 1989) as "cultural discount"—the more culturally distant a product, the lower the demand and lower the price that can be asked.

These factors are more important than the particular technology involved, and the "communications revolution" has not made a great deal of difference, despite early dreams of transnational television resulting from satellite transmission. This is true even in the densely populated patchwork of many national media systems to be found in Western Europe, where a project for pan-European television titled "Television Without Frontiers" has made little progress.

The third type of transnational flow is a *bilateral* one in which audiences find an unintended source of supply across their immediate frontiers—this applies especially to television. It can be considered as a "spillover effect." Examples are offered by Canadian reception of American television, Irish of British, Austrian of German, and so on. Such audiences may not be intended or even wanted by the originating source and country. The cultural consequences are often regretted or disputed, as with Canada and the United States and in other cases where small countries are overshadowed by big neighbors sharing the same language.

Sometimes bilateral flows are actually planned and are carried out for economic or political objectives. Luxembourg is an example of a country in which broadcasting to neighbors has long been a major national industry. In such cases, there may be legal and commercial problems arising because of copyright, advertising control, and principles of national sovereignty and identity. In the European Union, the transnational Television Directive is a legal agreement designed to resolve some of these problems and to facilitate bilateral flow.

International communication flows are complex and the term *transnational audience* has multiple referents. It is doubtful if there is any widespread (or increasing) subjective audience awareness of such an audience identity, although the media themselves increasingly draw attention to the phenomenon. None of the situations outlined above is completely novel, although the possibility of their occurrence is somewhat greater than in the past. The true extent of international audience formation is largely unknown, because it is virtually unmeasurable or because there is insufficient vested interest in trying to measure it.

Conclusion

It is clear that the seemingly simple notions of "being in the audience" and "in contact with media" are deceptive, and the aspiration to pin down the *reach* of a medium, channel, or message is ultimately likely to be frustrated. With all the developments of research technique, there can never be more than a very approximate estimate of who was (or is being) reached, where, and under what circumstances and in what state of mind.

FIVE

Principles of Audience Formation and Continuity

The "Why" of Media Use

Those whose task it is to smooth the path of the media machine must pay close attention to the causes and dynamics of audience formation. In circumstances of intense intermedia competition and constant change it is not enough to have "historical" knowledge of audience size and composition. It is also necessary to anticipate and lead audience tastes and interests. This is primarily a matter of professional skill, intuition, and luck, but it can be assisted by a deeper knowledge of what makes audiences tick. Theorists are also interested in what motivates individuals to join audiences and in the balance of forces that maintains them.

Broadcast television still attracts the highest share of audience research, partly because of its size and economic and social significance, but also because, without the help of research, its audience is less easy to track and to account for than audiences for most other media. Since many households share the same receiver for several or many channels, there is always a large traffic moving in and out of any particular program or channel audience. Advertisers and planners need to know as much as possible about these movements on a more or less continuous basis. The need to know about television audiences has been increased by the growth of cable and satellite delivery systems, the diffusion of recording equipment and of additional receivers, plus the arrival of other new media. The chances for the audience to escape from their monitors (in both senses of the word) have increased and are increasing.

Even so, questions of choice and constancy do arise with media other than television. Newspapers seek to attract new subscribers, win readers from rivals, and cement the loyalty of existing readers. Newly launched newspapers try to recruit and hold a regular readership base. Promoters of books and records want to understand their potential audience in order to market their products and maintain loyalty to performers and authors. From a theoretical point of view, there is just as much interest in knowing why and how people choose their books, periodicals, newspapers, rented videos, and music cassettes as in their television choices.

In line with earlier remarks, we can approach the question either from the "side" of the audience, asking what influences individual choices and behaviors, or from the side of the media, asking what factors of content, presentation, and circumstance help to draw and keep audience attention. There is no sharp division between the two, since questions of personal motivation cannot be answered without some reference to media products and contents.

We can also choose to follow one or more of the audience research schools described earlier (Chapter 2), each of which suggests a somewhat different kind of explanation for media use behavior. The structural tradition emphasizes the media system and the social system as primary determinants. The behavioral (functionalist) approach takes individual needs, motives, and circumstances as the starting point, while the sociocultural approach emphasizes the particular context in which an audience member is located and the way in which media alternatives are valued and given meaning. As we have seen, each approach has different theoretical foundations and entails different kinds of research strategy and methods. This chapter is written without making an exclusive choice among the three, since the aim is to assemble as broad a picture as possible.

A good deal is known about the general factors shaping audience behavior, which is usually marked by considerable stability and predictability (see, e.g., Zillman & Bryant, 1985). Broad patterns of attention to media change only slowly and usually for obvious reasons, such as a change in media structure (e.g., the rise of a new medium) or because of some wider social change (e.g., the development of a youth culture or the transition from communism to capitalism). There are always random influences and chance combinations of factors, but audience research is mostly a matter of routine recording of very predictable outcomes. Such mystery as there is relates to questions of detailed choice within a media sector, between channels or products, or concerning the success or failure of some specific innovation or item of content. If there were no mystery, the media business would not be as risky as it is and every film, song, book, or show could be a hit.

These remarks are a reminder that there has always been something of a disjunction between the *general* pattern of mass media use and what happens on a day-to-day basis. In one respect this can be understood as the difference between an average based on extensive aggregate data and observation of a single case, where the case might be one day's pattern or one person's habitual media use. As individuals, we usually have a fairly stable pattern of media preferences, choices, and time use, but each day's media experience is unique and affected by varying and unpredictable circumstances.

In the following sections we look at some alternative theoretical models for accounting for the recruitment and composition of media audiences.

A Structural Approach to Audience Formation

The basic premise, as indicated already, is that media use is largely shaped by certain relatively constant elements of social structure and media structure. Social structure refers to "social facts," such as those of education, income, gender, place of residence, position in the life-cycle, and so on, that have a strong determining influence on general outlook and behavior. Media structure refers to the relatively constant array of channels, choices, and content that is available in a given place and time. The media system responds to pressures and to feedback from audiences, so as to maintain a stable self-regulating balance between supply and demand.

The processes at work are sketched in a model (Figure 5.1), slightly adapted from Weibull (1985), that depicts the relationship between that habitual pattern of media use behavior and the particular choices, for instance on a given day. In Figure 5.1, the upper section shows an individual's habitual pattern of media use as an outcome of two main factors that themselves reflect the overall social structure. One is the more or less fixed *social situation* in which a person is located along with the associated media-related *needs* (e.g., for certain information, relaxation, social contact, etc.). The second factor (shown as "mass media structure") consists of the available media possibilities in the particular place, given a person's economic and educational circumstances. Between them, these two factors lead not only to a regular pattern of behavior, but also to a fairly constant disposition, tendency, or "set," which is called a person's "media orientation." This is a joint outcome of social background and past media experience and takes the form of an affinity for certain media, specific preferences and interests, habits of use, expectations of what the media are good for, and so on (see McDonald, 1990; McLeod & McDonald, 1985).

This provides the connection to what is contained in the lower part of the figure. Here we find the particular daily situation in which specific choices of media and content are made. These are likely to be influenced by three main variables: the specific daily menu of content on offer and the form of presentation (shown as "media content"); the circumstances of the moment (e.g., amount of free time, availability to attend, range of alternative activities available) (labeled as "individual's circumstances"); and the social context of choice and use (e.g., the influence of family and friends). Up to a point, what happens on a day-to-day basis is predictable from a person's media orientation, but the specifics are contingent on many unpredictable circumstances.

Weibull (1985) has tested this model with newspaper reading and he concluded that "when an individual is highly motivated to obtain specific gratifications [e.g., a particular item of sports news] he or she is less affected by media structure. . . . Individuals with less interest in the media seem to be more influenced by specific contents or by content composition" (p. 145). This is a reminder of the high degree of freedom we all have in principle to deviate from the general patterns arising from social and media structure. It also helps to explain why evidence about general tastes and preferences does not have a very high degree of short-term or individual predictive value.

While many features of daily media use can be traced back to their origins in social and media structure, this kind of model is no more than a preliminary orientation to the question of actual audience formation, which is based on many personal choices. It does have the advantage, however, of showing the connection between a media system (or structure) and an individual audience member's social position. The media system reflects the given facts of a society (e.g., economic, cultural, and geographical conditions) and also re-

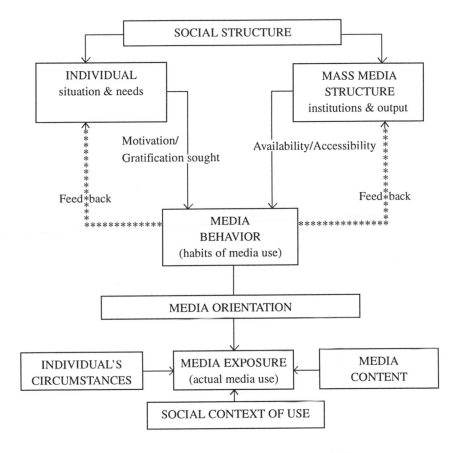

Figure 5.1. A Structural Model of Media Use (after Weibull, 1985).
NOTE: Used by permission.

sponds to audience demands that are partly determined by social background factors, partly idiosyncratic and contingent.

A Functionalist Model: The Uses and Gratifications Approach

The idea that media use depends on the perceived satisfactions, needs, wishes, or motives of the prospective audience member is almost as old as media research itself. As noted in Chapter 2, audiences are often formed on the basis of similarities of individual need, interest, and taste. Many of these appear to have a social or psychological origin. Typical of such "needs" are those for information, relaxation, companionship, diversion, or "escape." Audiences for particular media and kinds of media content can often be typified according to such broad motivational types. The approach has also been applied to studying the appeal of new electronic media (Perse, 1990) and even to uses of the telephone (Dimmick, Sikard, & Patterson, 1994). Relative affinity with different media is associated with differences of expectation and gratifications sought.

This way of thinking belongs to a research school that became known as the "uses and gratifications approach," the origins of which lie in the search for explanations of the great appeal of certain staple media contents. The central question posed is: *Why* do people use media and what do they use them for? Functionalist sociology (see Wright, 1974) viewed the media as serving various needs of the society—such as, for cohesion, cultural continuity, social control, and for a large circulation of public information of all kinds. This, in turn, presupposes that individuals also use media for related purposes such as personal guidance, relaxation, adjustment, information, and identity formation.

The first such research dates from the early 1940s and focused on the reasons for the popular appeal of different radio programs, especially "soap operas" and quizzes, and also of daily newspaper reading (Lazarsfeld & Stanton, 1944, 1949). These studies led to some unexpected findings, for instance that daytime radio soap operas, although often dismissed as superficial and mindless stories to fill time, were often found significant by their (women) listeners. They provided a source of advice and support, a role model of housewife and mother, or an occasion for emotional release through laughter or tears (Herzog, 1953; Warner & Henry, 1948). From talking to newspaper readers, it was also discovered that newspapers were more than just sources of useful information, but also important for giving readers a sense of security, shared topics of conversation, and a structure to the daily routine (Berelson, 1949).

Uses and Gratifications Rediscovered

The basic assumptions of the approach when it was rediscovered and elaborated 20 years later (in the 1960s and 1970s) were that: (a) media and content choice is generally rational and directed toward certain specific goals and satisfactions (thus the audience is active and audience formation can be logically explained); (b) audience members are conscious of the media-related needs that arise in personal (individual) and social (shared) circumstances and can voice these in terms of motivations; (c) broadly speaking, personal utility is a more significant determinant of audience formation than aesthetic or cultural factors; and (d) all or most of the relevant factors for audience formation (motives, perceived or obtained satisfactions, media choices, background variables) can, in principle, be measured.

A version of the process of media selection was set out by Katz, Blumler, and Gurevitch (1974) as being concerned with: "(1) the social and psychological origins of (2) needs that generate (3) expectations of (4) the mass media or other sources which lead to (5) differential exposure (or engaging in other activities), resulting in (6) need gratification and (7) other consequences" (p. 20). In a leading contemporary model of the media use process, Rosengren (1974) began with the concept of basic human needs or requirements, and described a sequence in which some of these would be experienced as "problems," generating a search for possible "solutions," leading to "motives," some of which would lead to media use, others to nonmedia forms of solution (e.g., personal social contact or going out).

This branch of theory of media use is individualistic and behavioristic in formulation, although it also implies that audiences will have some collective properties, especially shared sets of expected satisfactions and a similar range of needs deriving from their social background (Babrow, 1988; Lichtenstein & Rosenfeld, 1983; McQuail, 1984). These theoretical assumptions together support the general proposition that the *more* and the *more salient* are the self-perceived needs, the more likely a person is to attend to the media. They also presume a logical connection between audience background experience and the characteristics of the specific content chosen.

A longer-term aim of the research school was to reach some general theoretical framework within which to place the many particular findings about audience motivations. For example, von Feilitzen (1976) summed up the main reasons for (Swedish) children's use of the media in terms of the following main headings:

- Entertainment and emotional satisfactions
- Informational and cognitive needs
- Social needs—Identity, talking with others

▦ Nonsocial needs, especially related to "escape," being alone, and mood management (see also Katz & Foulkes, 1962; Zillman & Bryant, 1985)

▦ Needs related to the mode of consumption and the medium itself (e.g., book, radio, etc.) that hold certain intrinsic satisfactions for the user (see also Brown, 1976)

McQuail, Blumler, and Brown (1972), after studying a number of different radio and TV programs in Britain, proposed the following scheme of *media-person interactions* (a term that reflects the dual origin of the media gratification concept), which capture the most important media satisfactions:

1. *Diversion:* Escape from routine or problems; emotional release
2. *Personal relationships:* Companionship; social utility
3. *Personal identity:* Self-reference; reality exploration; value reinforcement
4. *Surveillance* (forms of information seeking)

A more psychological version of the theory of audience motivation was suggested by McGuire (1974), based on general theory of human needs. He distinguished first between cognitive and affective needs, then added three further dimensions: "active" versus "passive" initiation; "external" versus "internal" goal orientation; and orientation to "growth" or to "stability." When interrelated, these factors yield 16 different types of motivation that apply to media use. Examples include the "search for cognitive consistency" by reading a newspaper (this belongs to a cognitive, active, external, stability-oriented type) or the motive for watching television drama "in order to find models of personal behavior" (an affective, active, internal, growth-oriented type). In the nature of psychological theory of this kind, the media user is unlikely to be conscious of the underlying causes of motivations. Even so, there has been some research that shows a relationship between the McGuire factors and different motivational patterns of television use (Conway & Rubin, 1991).

Comment and Criticism

There has been rather little successful prediction or causal explanation of media choice and use as a result of research based on these theories although the approach seems to work best in relation to specific types of content, for instance selective attention to political content (Blumler & McQuail, 1968) or news (Levy, 1978; Palmgreen, Wenner, & Rayburn, 1980), or erotica (Perse,

1994). In general, the connection between attitude toward the media and media use behavior is weak and the direction of the relationship is uncertain. Typologies of "motives" often fail to match patterns of actual selection or use, and it is hard to find a logical and consistent relation among the three sequentially ordered factors of: *liking/preference;* actual *choosing;* and subsequent *evaluation.*

There is little empirical evidence that media use does in general begin with an experience of a problem or lead to the solution of one, although we can usually find occasions when this does apply. It is true that when people are asked about their motives for media use, they can reproduce or recognize many of the expected kinds of "motives" that have been mentioned. This allows audiences to be described in functionalist terms and this is how audiences often seem to make sense of their own media use, when pressed to do so. In general, however, the "uses and gratifications" approach overestimates the rationality and activity of audience use behavior. Most actual audiences also turn out to be composed of people with varied, overlapping, and not always consistent expectations and subjective motives.

The extent to which audience behavior is guided by specific and conscious motives has always been in dispute. Babrow (1988) shares the doubts and has proposed that we think more in terms of "interpretive frameworks," based on experience. Thus some audience choice is meaningful in terms of such frameworks, whereas other exposure is based only on habit and reflex and may be considered unmotivated (Rubin, 1984). These ideas are in line with the concept of "media orientation" introduced earlier in this chapter and the idea of a general preference set included in Figure 5.3 below.

It is unclear whether the relative lack of success of the approach results mainly from methodological weakness (there are many measurement pitfalls and many interrelated factors to measure) or whether it simply reflects a reality in which individual media selection and use is actually very circumstantial, inconsistent, and weakly motivated. Probably both explanations are valid, although the latter may be more significant than the former. If so, there are severe limits to the chances of ever reaching an adequate theory of audience motivation.

In discussing the status of uses and gratifications theory, Blumler (1985) made a distinction between social origins and ongoing social experience. Some kinds of social origin (e.g., relating to education and social class) are associated in a predictable way with constraints on the range of choice as well as with compensatory, adjustment-oriented media expectations and uses.

However, certain aspects of ongoing experience and current social situation are much less predictable in their consequences for media choice and use. They often go with "facilitatory" media uses—with positive choice, and application, of media for personally chosen ends. This means that media use is an outcome of forces in society, of the personal biography of the individual, and also of immediate circumstances. The *causes* of audience formation are located in the past as well as in the very immediate present and at points in between. It is not surprising that attempts at general *explanation* of actual audience realities have had so little success.

Expectancy-Value Theory

Essential to most theory concerning personal motivations for media use is the idea that the media offer rewards that are expected (thus predicted) by potential members of an audience on the basis of relevant past experience. These rewards can be thought of as experienced psychological effects that are valued by individuals (they are sometimes called media "gratifications"). Such rewards can be derived from media use as such (e.g., "having a good read") or from certain favorite genres (e.g., detective stories) or actual items of content (a particular film), and they provide guidance (or feedback) for subsequent choices, adding to the stock of media-relevant information. A model of the process involved has been proposed by Palmgreen and Rayburn (1985), based on the principle that attitudes (toward media) are an outcome of empirically located beliefs and also of values (and personal preferences). The resulting "expectancy-value" model is depicted in Figure 5.2.

In general, the model expresses the proposition that media use is accounted for by a combination of *perception* of benefits offered by the medium and the differential *value* of these benefits for the individual audience member. This helps to cover the fact that media use is shaped by *avoidance* as well as by varying degrees of positive choice among the potential gratifications expected from the media. The model distinguishes between expectation (gratifications sought) and satisfaction (gratifications obtained), and identifies an *increment* over time from media use behavior. Thus, where GO (gratifications obtained) is noticeably higher than GS (gratifications sought) we are likely to be dealing with situations of high audience satisfaction and high scores for appreciation and attention. The reverse pattern can also occur, providing clues to falling circulation, sales, or ratings, and channel switching in the case of

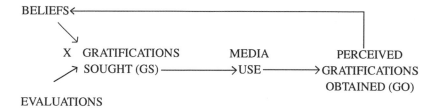

The elements in the model are formally related as follows:

$$GS_i = b_i e_i$$

where GS_i = the ith gratification sought from some media object X (medium, program, or content type);

b_i = the belief (subjective probability) that X possesses some attribute or that a behavior related to X will have a particular outcome; and

e_i = the affective evaluation of the particular attribute or outcome.

Figure 5.2. An Expectancy-Value Model of Media Gratifications Sought and Obtained (Palmgreen & Rayburn, 1985)

television. This theoretical refinement has not altered the fact that audience motivational theory is not easy to translate into a sharp empirical tool.

A Nonfunctionalist Alternative to Explaining Media Use

There have been other ways of theorizing the origins of audience that avoid a number of the functionalist and behaviorist assumptions as outlined here. For instance, Renckstorf (1989) has proposed a "social action" model in which media choices are viewed as the outcome of personal social projects, influenced by a definition of the situation and by perceptions of "problems" (for a summary see McQuail & Windahl, 1993). Media use may sometimes be considered as a motivated solution to a perceived problem, but more often and more probably it is part of an everyday routine that can take on a wide variety of definitions. The emphasis is on interpreting media use as meaningful in a certain social situation, rather than on trying to find a structural or behavioral *cause*. The relevant school of sociology is not functionalism, but phenomenology and symbolic interactionism (see McQuail & Gurevitch, 1974; Renckstorf, McQuail, & Jankowski, 1996).

A "Pragmatic" Model
of Audience Choice

The above discussion has already provided us with a guide to the main different influences on media choice and audience formation. It is useful to try to combine these into a single heuristic model that provides a guide to understanding the sequential process of audience formation. The main entries in the model (Figure 5.3) operate either "on the audience side" of the media-person interaction or on the "media side." Although described separately, the two sets of factors are not independent of each other, but the result of a continuing process of mutual orientation and adjustment. The form of the model as presented here was influenced initially by the work of Webster and Wakshlag (1983), who sought to explain television viewer choice in a similar way. The version shown here is intended, in principle, to apply to all mass media and not just television. First the main explanatory factors can be introduced.

"Audience Side" Factors

1. *Social background and milieu,* especially as reflected in social class, education, religious, cultural, political, and family environment and region or locality of residence. We can also refer here to what Bourdieu (1984) calls "cultural capital"—learned cultural skills and tastes, often transmitted inter-generationally by way of family, education, and the class system.

2. *Personal attributes* of age, gender, family position, study and work situation, level of income; also lifestyle, if relevant.

3. *Media-related needs,* of the kind discussed above, for such personal benefits as company, distraction, information, and so on. These needs are widely experienced, but the particular balance among them depends on personal background and circumstances.

4. *Personal tastes and preferences* for certain genres, formats, or specific items of content.

AudiENCE SidE

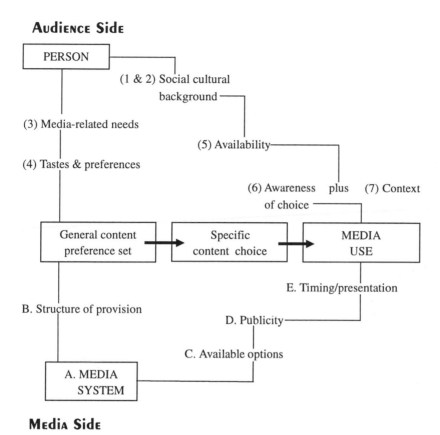

Figure 5.3. An Integrated Model of the Process of Media Choice

5. *General habits of leisure-time media use* and availability to be in the audience at a particular time. Because media are used in space as well as time, availability also refers to being in the appropriate places to receive (e.g., at home, in trains, driving, etc.). Availability also refers to the economic potential to be in an audience, for instance being able and willing to pay the price of a cinema ticket or a music recording.

6. *Awareness* of the choices available and the amount and kind of information possessed also play a part in audience formation. More active audience members can be expected to plan their media use accordingly.

7. *Specific context of use* varies according to medium but generally refers to sociability and location of use. Most relevant is whether one is alone or in company (friends, family, others). Where media are used (e.g., at home, work, traveling, in a cinema, etc.) can also influence the character of the experience as well as the process of choice making.

8. *Chance* often plays a part in media exposure and its intervention reduces the ability to really *explain* choice or audience composition.

"Media Side" Factors

A. The Media System. Preferences and choices are influenced by the makeup of the (national) media system (number, reach, and type of media available) and by the specific characteristics of different media outlets.

B. Structure of Media Provision. This refers to the general pattern of what the media provide in a given society, which exerts a long-term influence on audience expectations.

C. Available Content Options. The specific formats and genres that are on offer to the potential audience at particular times and places.

D. Media Publicity. This includes advertising and image making by the media on their own behalf as well as intensive marketing of some media products.

E. Timing and Presentation. Media selection and use are likely to be influenced by specific strategies of timing, scheduling, placement or design of content, or media message according to competitive audience-gaining strategies.

Figure 5.3 represents the general process of choice making, in which influences of both kinds (from society and from media) are shown sequentially according to their relative "distance" from the moment of choice or attention (MEDIA USE). Most distant (and more or less fixed) are social and cultural background and (for most adults, at least) general sets of tastes and preferences, likes and interests. Thus our social background has a strongly orienting and dispositional influence on our choice behavior. The other, almost equally distant (but less constant) factor is the general makeup of different media and the mix of genres, of which we have accumulated knowledge and experience. There is both a cognitive and an evaluative aspect to our dispositions (see the expectancy-value model above).

Personal knowledge of this kind and the related attitudes shape our tastes and preferences. The combination of the two (perception and evaluation) leads to a GENERAL CONTENT PREFERENCE SET. This is a hypothetical construct, but it shows up in consistent and thus predictable patterns of choice making and also in more or less coherent patterns and types of media usage (these are close to what are sometimes called "taste cultures"). We can think of it in terms of the "repertoire" of available sources and content types with which we are familiar and from which we make actual choices (see Heeter, 1988). It is also very close to Weibull's media orientation in the structural model (see Figure 5.1) and includes affinity for media as well as for types of content. Patterns of choice making are, of course, always adapted according to changes in circumstances and experience with the media. There is a continuous process of response, feedback, learning, and evaluation.

At a point much closer in time or place to MEDIA USE, the circumstances of the potential audience member and the availability of the media coincide, resulting in actual audiences. These are never fully predictable, although the broad shape in aggregate terms is, as noted above, rather constant. It is the internal composition that is always shifting, since individual choice behavior is affected by circumstances.

Tastes, Preferences, and Interests

It is easy to lose sight of the fact that audiences form because people are attracted to different kinds of content. We make choices according to fine distinctions of personal preference, even if these are hard to put into words. Normally, media choice does not have to be articulated. Media preferences may be related to social background, but they are also specific and unpredictable. Individual media tastes are also often very enduring once they have been formed in childhood and youth (Himmelweit & Swift, 1976). The appeal of certain staple items (or genres) of media content (such as news, film, music, entertainment, drama) cuts across the many differences of social and cultural background, and the distribution of such preferences also varies in broadly predictable ways. In general, for instance, there is more demand for amusement, vicarious excitement, or romantic stories than for education, religion, or pornography. Some types and specific items of content have only a restricted appeal.

Patterns of individual taste can be uncovered by empirical research. For instance, in their study of Swedish youth (aged 19-21), Johansson and Miegel (1992) explored attitudes toward music and established the existence of 12 main types (factors) derived from a larger set of 55 music genres. They looked at relations among preferences and values and other background variables. One important finding is that one popular category—"Mainstream" (pop and disco music)—indicates the "existence of a common cultural base for young people in Sweden" (p. 169). Three other types were likely to differentiate taste: jazz, opera and musicals, and "socially conscious" music. Several other studies have uncovered clear patterns in musical preferences (e.g., Christensen & Peterson, 1988; G. H. Lewis, 1992; Robinson & Fink, 1986; Roe, 1985).

A similar analysis of film preferences (Johansson & Miegel, 1992) showed an equally wide range of appreciation of different genres, categorized according to nine different factors. Certain genres were largely rejected, including pornographic, violent, socially controversial, experimental, psychological, or poetic films. An important finding was that, in contrast with musical taste, there is much more differentiation according to social status and gender (thus, in general, "positional" rather than value-related variables are more significant). The specifics are not very surprising, but these findings reinforce the view that traditional patterns of taste do persist and are probably reinforced rather than challenged by media supply and accompanying marketing strategies (Negus, 1992).

News, whether printed or broadcast, still constitutes a major category of media content. It is clear that there are widely differing degrees of interest in the topics of news and that these differences are related both to demographic factors and also to having an intrinsic interest in media news as such. Research by the National Advertising Bureau (NAB; 1984) indicated that for a sample of American readers the most interesting categories of news were, in this order: international; sports; local community; economic. But it has also appeared from other research (e.g., Robinson & Levy, 1986) that the properties of individual news "stories" can easily override general categories. The results of research can depend on how questions are asked. It looks as if social desirability influences the response to questions of this kind.

Attending to news is influenced not only by an abstract set of "interests," but also by an assessment of relevance to the audience member. As another newspaper reader survey has shown (National Advertising Bureau [NAB], 1982), news attention is shaped by the different *roles* that audience members occupy in everyday life, for instance those of: family member; citizen; worker; consumer; spender of leisure time. Each of these is associated with certain patterns of interest at certain times, but they are not all exclusive. At different times we follow the requirements of different roles. Audience attention to news is structured according to an elaborate set of prior interests and needs that guide choice. These "mental sets" are also very influential in comprehending and processing news content (see Graber, 1984; Robinson & Levy, 1986), although this topic goes beyond the scope of the present discussion.

There are obvious regularities in the pattern of demand, but personal tastes or actual media preferences defy explanation or prediction. We can broadly estimate demand for staple fare, but have still to regard cultural taste and preference as something of a black box, beyond the reach of communication science. The best that can be done is to describe patterns as they appear at a given moment in time and in a particular cultural setting. The scale of this task may be one reason why the analysis of tastes, preferences, and interests has been neglected in audience research.

There have been numerous attempts to establish typologies of audience members (especially in relation to television) according to preference and pattern of use, beyond the relatively straightforward matter of varying degree of use (e.g., "heavy" vs. "light" viewers), although nearly always this variable contributes powerfully to other dimensions of content chosen or degree of selectivity. In the "uses and gratifications" tradition, the distinction between those seeking more information and those looking for entertainment has been a crude but robust discriminator (e.g., Rubin, 1983), as has that between planned (instrumental) and habitual (ritual) use reported by Rubin (1984). Other relevant dimensions relate to the degree of selectivity (Weiman et al., 1992), channel, or genre loyalty (Hawkins, Reynolds, & Pingree, 1991). Types of viewers and listeners can always be found, but the boundaries are usually very blurred and the identities of types found are indistinct (Van den Bulk, 1995).

Even categorizing content in a way that reflects differences of audience taste and preference is not easy. It has proved difficult to improve on the conventional categories of content used by the different media industries themselves for purposes of audience recruitment (by publicity and information) or accounting. These categories are so widely, if imprecisely, known by the public that they inevitably influence the perceptions of audience members and their responses to survey questions. Even when researchers want to find some more discriminating alternative for describing audience tastes, they cannot get around this obstacle.

Audience Flow

One of the practical reasons for trying to describe media content stems from a continual preoccupation by media planners, especially in television, with the question of recruiting and holding of audiences. As Webster (1986) points out, there are three different questions that arise in relation to the "flow" of the television audience. One is the question of *inheritance*—the transfer of part of an audience from a program to the one immediately following. Second, there is *repeat viewing*—the degree to which the same people watch different episodes of a serial or series from day to day or week to week. The third concerns channel *loyalty*—the degree to which viewers disproportionately watch the programs of one channel. Each of these represents one of the ways in which programmers hope to capture and keep a larger share of the audience. Somewhat similar questions can be posed for other media, especially with respect to loyalty.

There is plenty of empirical evidence of inheritance effects—a disproportionate and often predictable share of the viewers of a given program stay on to view the next program, whatever its actual content (see Emmett, 1972). One obvious explanation lies in viewer inertia and passivity—for part of the audience viewing is not content-specific, but a generalized activity, a way of passing time. More difficult to interpret is the outcome of group or family viewing, when a succeeding program just happens to suit one person rather than others or when continuing minimizes conflict. A more "active" explanation of inheritance derives from channel loyalty, which implies a constancy of preference and surrender of judgment to the favorite channel. Sometimes a channel is trusted to provide the best *mix* of content and is a favorite collective choice for this reason. Inheritance depends on continued audience availability. After reaching an evening peak, there is gradually less of the television audience to inherit.

The question of repeat viewing, its degree and explanation, has been much contested in television research (Cooper, 1996), although the strategy of trying to retain viewers' loyalty by way of long-running series and horizontal or strip programming (same program each day at the same time) is one of the favorite weapons in the armory of programmers. There are a number of other factors that programmers use in order to increase short-term loyalty (for a model of the process, see Cooper, 1993). As described by Webster and Lichty (1991), strategies include: "lead-in," when a strong program can be expected to retain part of its audience; "hammocking," when programs with a weaker audience pull are inserted between two "strong" shows; "block-programming"— putting similar content shows together; and "tent-poling"—locating a strong show between two weaker ones.

Barwise and Ehrenberg (1988) have sought to establish and explain the regularities of repeat viewing, especially with respect to series or serials. Their evidence has consistently shown rather low but also predictable levels of repeat viewing in Britain and the United States. Typically, no more than 40% or 50% of an audience is likely to be present in the succeeding episode of a series or serial, and the actual proportion is normally a function of the total audience size for both episodes. The degree of program loyalty varies according to the type of program and the time interval between one episode and another.

Although Barwise and Ehrenberg tend to stress the relative lack of specific *content-related* effects on viewing choices (as distinct from the influence of viewing habits), they emphasize that some program loyalty does exist. The probability that a given viewer of a given series will view the next episode (even if only 50%) is normally a good deal higher than the probability that a *nonviewer* of the given episode will watch the next one. Those who miss episodes are not necessarily lost to a series. Virtually no one watches all the episodes of a series, although *cumulative* audiences (or reach) for a series can be very high.

Barwise and Ehrenberg (1988) give the example (not untypical) of the British classic drama series *Brideshead Revisited,* which had a total reach (at least 1 of the 11 episodes seen) of 26 million viewers (60% of the U.K. adult population). However, of this total, only 3% saw all the episodes and 46% saw only one or two. The relatively high degree of discontinuity in watching drama serials has something to do with the circumstances of collective viewing in families and with competing choices. But there is also evidence of low motivation to "keep up" with story lines. Channel loyalty in relation to *television* is not easy to separate from inheritance effects or audience flow. The lead-in effects from one program to another on the same channel have been measured and appear usually to be of short duration. The phenomenon of loyalty can also be measured as an attitude, and stable preferences do exist and are correlated with choice behavior. The image or profile of different channels as well as taste and socioeconomic background play a part. Public Television in the United States is, for instance, differently positioned by its audience than regular network channels. The same applies to the BBC in Britain compared to ITV, and in several European countries there are other bases (e.g., region or politics) for differences of perception and preference. The rise of more content-specific television channels, whether free or subscription, is likely to give a new meaning to television channel loyalty, making it more akin to the selection of a special interest magazine. Questions of attraction and inheritance also arise with print media. Newspapers and magazines are put together so as to maximize internal inheritance effects and advertisers depend on a high degree of transfer of reader attention from one item to another. *Reader* loyalty (for newspapers and magazines) has a somewhat different meaning, as well as being much more pronounced, than has channel loyalty for television. The essence of (daily) newspaper loyalty, for instance, is a continued subscription (or regular purchase) by a person or household to the same title. Being a "loyal reader" usually follows from this.

The commitment differs from that of the loyal television channel follower in several ways. First, it is likely to be much more consistent and exclusive and carries with it an element of personal commitment. Newspaper choice costs money and "switching" may also take an effort. Second, the opportunities for switching are more infrequent—once a day is usually the maximum frequency possible, and relatively few people anywhere take more than one newspaper. Third, the commitment to the newspaper has traditionally derived from much deeper roots—those of community, politics, social class, religion. A newspaper is often a social marker and a reflection and reinforcer of one's identity and self-image. The readership of many newspapers still reflects membership of a "public" or a social or political identity in "civil society." Many newspapers have long and continuous histories, with established traditions, despite changes with the times.

Because of all these things, reader loyalty can extend over many years, transmitted intergenerationally, more likely to be upset by the takeover or disappearance of the title for commercial reasons than by the disloyalty of readers. On a practical note, there are many cities and regions without a real alternative newspaper, so that title loyalty is almost obligatory. Loyalty to a newspaper in a situation of no choice has a lower and different significance than in a situation of press diversity.

In the ideal-typical case of the loyal reader, we are dealing with a special case of fandom, cemented by social and other ties. Here, the concept of "activity" implies extensive reading, exclusivity of attention, reflection on and response to content (in conversation or by writing to the newspaper). Active and loyal readership entails the threat of giving up the subscription and indicates the existence of some measure of reader control.

For many purposes of media planning and presentation, editorial orientation to a specific social-demographic category (or more than one) or to a taste culture defined by interests and preferences is an available strategy. We can approach this topic by way of the concept of "inscribed reader" (Sparks & Campbell, 1987). This refers to the typical "addressee" (intended audience member) of a media channel that we can usually recognize from the content alone according to markers such as topic, taste, level of literacy, price, and various quality indicators. Also indicative is the kind of advertising carried, since this is very specifically tailored to an anticipated audience.

Targeting (and thus also inscription) by the media can take place by manipulation of place and time of appearance. Print media are sold at locations where they maximize the chance of being encountered by the intended type of consumer (airports, railway stations, street corners, etc.). Within the newspaper, reader attention can be manipulated by decisions about prominence and placement, thus exercising some control over what is likely to receive audience attention. Broadcasting can do the same by scheduling decisions, influencing the relative size of audiences for different kinds of content. It can also inscribe audiences by specific timing decisions. For instance, women audiences are defined by daytime programming, children by early evening offerings, younger people by late-night presentations, and so on.

Conclusion

The complexity and multiplicity of audience formation precludes any simple descriptions or single theoretical explanation. We can certainly conclude that audiences are rarely what they seem. They are often shifting aggregates without clear boundaries. Motives and orientations are always mixed. Sometimes there are no motives. Even if motives were clearer and less mixed they would not be "readable" from the content alone, although in an efficient media market we may suppose that content and audience composition are well matched. There are enormous built-in uncertainties that cannot be eliminated. Nevertheless, within the complexity and seeming confusion there are some islands of stability and order—occasions where people and media meet to mutual satisfaction and stay with each other. However, this state is one that, by definition, is not easy to achieve by manipulation and publicity, but comes either from genuine social needs or from chance conjunctures of media creativity and public taste.

SIX

Audience Practices: Social Uses of the Media

Media Use and Everyday Life

The approaches described in the two previous chapters have problematized the "audience" as an uncertain outcome of many individual acts of more or less motivated choice. These acts can, up to a point, be accounted for by a number of interacting causal factors—the pushes of individual needs and social pressures, the disposition of circumstances, the relative attraction of particular media offerings. This way of formulating the problem stems from the motives that have guided most audience research: meeting the needs of media industries or the aims of media propagandists and responding to public concerns about harmful media effects.

From each of these perspectives, media use tends to be viewed as a causally motivated sequence of behavior, which is open to both prediction and modification in some relevant way. In the same vein, Webster and Phalen (1994) pointed to three main audience models in communication policy that position the audience respectively as: "victim" (in the effect model); "consumer" (in the marketplace model); and "coin of exchange" (in the commodity model). Whatever the model, the audience in these conceptualizations is more a statistical abstraction than a human constellation.

87

More recently, an audience research school has developed that has tried to avoid and even counter this way of looking at audiences by treating media use as an integral part of something more fundamental, namely the patterns of everyday social interaction and experience that not only influence specific media behaviors but that also govern the meaning that media use has for its audiences (Moores, 1993; Silverstone, 1994). The general term *reception research* refers to this new school of audience thinking according to which "audiencehood" is itself a learned and varied form of cultural and social practice.

The origins of this school lie in a critical reaction against manipulative perspectives on the mass audience and against the notion that gaining the attention of the audience also means gaining control over it. They are also to be found in culturalist theory, which revalues and seeks to re-empower the many (weaker) minorities and subgroups in society whose uses of media are not in line with any project of social control or hegemony or with media industry priorities. Reception research has consistently distanced itself from uses and gratifications research for a number of reasons, but especially because of the latter's perceived functionalist and behaviorist bias (see Elliott, 1974; Morley, 1992). The elements that have been forged together in reception theory comprise a significant reorientation to audiencehood as an aspect of everyday social experience (Bausinger, 1984).

A Misleading Model of Media Use

It had not escaped early audience researchers that media use was shaped by circumstances of time and place, and by social and cultural habits. People joined audiences for various social reasons (e.g., for conversation or organizing daily routine), as much as for some communicative value or purpose (such as learning from the news). Eliot Freidson (1953), for instance, emphasized the group character of much actual media experience (in contrast to what the theory of mass behavior proposed), drawing on contemporary evidence of film and broadcast audiences. He wrote:

> Much audience behavior, then, takes place in a complex network of local social activity. Certain time of day, certain days, certain seasons are the appropriate times for engaging in particular activities connected with various

mass media. The individual is frequently accompanied by others of his social
group . . . [and] . . . participates in an interpersonal grid of spectators who
discuss the meaning of past experience with mass communication and the
anticipated significance of future experience. (p. 310)

However, it is true that early audience research had been framed in the
shadow of a model of communication as a linear process of transmission of
"messages" that privileged message "content" and its "impact" and treated
audience "exposure" as an aggregate of unrelated individual selections. The
important thing was for messages to be consciously received, registered, and
effective (see Chapter 4 under "A Generalized View of Media Reach and
Impact"). The features of social life that "got in the way" of this were either
to be treated as "noise," interference, or as irritating inconveniences in the
measurement process. Seemingly "unmotivated" behavior was often disregarded as without meaning. The view of the audience that accompanied the
transmission model was such that audiences could best be studied in a
laboratory (should that be feasible), leaving these "irrelevant" aspects out of
consideration.

We now know media use to be generally a very untidy, inefficient, and
chancy matter, with multiple meanings. The model of planned information
transmission is not only an abstraction, the process it represents is the
exception rather than the norm for most situations of mass communication. It
is therefore better forgotten as a means of understanding the audience, since
it does not even reflect the realities of media industry practice. Early forms of
media were often developed to fit in with the way of life (work, home, and
leisure) of particular social groups and to match the aspirations and attitudes
of potential audiences (Martell & McCall, 1964). The daily newspaper in its
content and production/distribution cycle was designed to match the routine
of the urban worker of the late 19th century. The weekly magazine for families
and women was designed to be picked up and casually read at odd moments
in the home. The cinema capitalized on the patterns of urban leisure, especially
of couples and groups of friends looking for convenient and cheap entertainment outside the home.

"Going to the movies" has nearly always been viewed more as a social
activity than as an occasion for seeing particular films (Handel, 1950). It
represents a continuation of the original "audience," made up of those who
went out to a public social event, usually in the company of others. The
occasion had a significance beyond that of any "message" communicated or

any individual gratification obtained. Seeing a "bad" movie could be just as satisfying as seeing a "good" one. Much the same could be said of radio, phonograph listening, and television viewing, although, unlike the cinema, these have nearly always taken a secondary place in complex patterns of family life.

"Watching television" is generally a more accurate description of what is going on than "watching television programs," but it too overstates the significance of the ubiquitous flickering screen. The extensive and detailed studies of time use by Kubey and Csikszentmihalyi (1991), based on self-reports, leave little doubt about the generally uninvolving and secondary character of television viewing, although this should not be confused with lack of significance. The untidiness and chanciness that characterize media use, as noted above, are in fact only a matter of perception, since there is always a certain logic, although not usually the logic of the "media exposure" model. The transmission model and the bias of behavioral science have tended to distort audience research, but so also has theory that conceptualizes the audience as a mass of isolated individuals "exposed" to extraneous influences.

Public and Private
Spheres of Media Use

As noted, certain forms of media use have a distinctly public character, both in the sense of taking place outside the home (as with cinema or concerts) and also in having a wider significance as a shared response to public performances and to public events. Saenz (1994) refers to the continued significance of a "widely shared, collectively appreciated performance, an immediate delivery . . . to a large and general audience" (p. 576). He adds, "the sense of performance and cultural currency in television programming constitutes an important dimension in viewers' appreciation of television drama as a prominent cultural event" (p. 576). The term *public* can have a reference to the type of content, the location of an event, and also to the degree of shared, collective, experience.

Mass media that are located in their use primarily in the home (especially television, video, music, and books) can be considered to bridge the gap between the private, domestic, world and the concerns and activities of the wider society. Under some conditions, being a member of an audience has the meaning of sharing in the wider life of society, while in other circumstances it is a self-initiated experience that may be entirely personal or shared only by a small circle of friends or family members. It is not so much the physical location of the audience experience (e.g., cinema and theater versus home) that matters as the definition of its meaning as more public or more private.

The public type of audiencehood is typified by occasions of consciously motivated attention to reports of events that are of wide social significance (e.g., election results, major disasters, world crises), or that involve watching major live sporting events on television (Rothenbuhler, 1987) or big entertainment events (e.g., live concerts). Public audience experience normally involves some degree of identification with a wider social grouping—whether defined as fans, or citizens, or a local population or a taste culture. It may also be experience associated with some more or less public role, for instance citizen, voter, or worker.

In their study of "media events," Dayan and Katz (1992) draw attention to a special category of occasions, when the media (especially television) unite a population in a near-ritual manner to celebrate and join in some wider national or global experience. Such media events are always special and constitute interruptions of routine. Aside from their significance, they are typically preplanned, remote, and live. The examples cited include the Olympic Games, Sadat's journey to Israel in 1978, major papal visits, coronations, and royal weddings. To be in the (media) audience for such events is to participate more fully in the public life of the nation or other significant membership group. This research reminds us again of the collective character of "audiencehood."

The private type of audience experience is constructed according to personal mood and circumstance and does not involve any reference to society or even to other people. When not purely introspective, it is likely to be concerned with self-comparison and matching with a media model, role, or personality in the search for an acceptable identity for public self-presentation. The difference between the public and the private type of audience experience depends on a combination of factors: the type of medium and content and the frame of mind of (or definition supplied by) the audience member. Expansion and development of media seem to be opening up relatively more possibilities for private audiencehood, by bringing more of media experience within the control of the individual to choose at will (see Neuman, 1991).

Subculture and Audience

Early critics of mass society theory pointed to the high degree of social differentiation of the seemingly homogeneous "mass" audience. The fact of receiving the same media channel or message cuts across, but does not weaken or override, the many prior differences of circumstance and outlook based on social class or life-cycle position. As media industries have developed and sought more new and "niche" audience markets, they have needed no persuasion on this point and have even entered the business of trying to define and create new social and cultural subgroups, based on taste or lifestyle, with which potential media consumers might identify. There is a continuous process of creating media-based styles or pseudo-identities that are intended to strike a responsive chord in an audience.

Nevertheless, media use is always likely to be shaped predominantly according to early experience and identifications forged in personal social life or in line with the social context of the moment. After the particular social milieu of one's family, comes the peer group of school classmates or neighborhood friends who influence taste and media consumption, especially in respect of music and television—the two most popular media for the young. There are many layers of differentiation, aside from the sometimes fine age-grading of youthful preferences (von Feilitzen, 1976) and the general separation out of a "youth culture" as distinct from that of adults. Young adult experience is reshaped by social contacts at work and in leisure. Such general environmental influences are cross-cut by many other specific factors, not least that of gender (van Zoonen, 1994).

There is much evidence that media use can play an important role in the expression and reinforcement of identity for subgroups of different kinds (Hebdige, 1978). This is not surprising, since media are part of "culture," but there is a particular point in noting the strong connection between more deviant and alternative subcultures in modern society and, especially, youth musical taste (Avery, 1979; Roe, 1992). The focus of resistance to dominant forces of society has often been musical and dance forms, which are appropriated by subcultures and become a symbol of resistance (Hall & Jefferson, 1975; Lull, 1992). Much modern music adopted by youth is anathema to parents, teachers, and to established society generally. Murdock and Phelps (1973), for instance, showed how young people expressed their distance from official school and middle-class values by way of musical tastes.

Lifestyle

The concept of "lifestyle" has often been used in describing and categorizing different patterns of media use, often as part of a constellation of other attitudes and behavior (e.g., Donohew, Palmgreen, & Rayburn, 1987; Eastman, 1979; Engel & Blackwell, 1982; Frank & Greenberg, 1980). The idea has a complex history, although its essence is familiar enough in common-sense ideas about the way in which social class differences influence taste, manners, dress, and behavior. The pioneering work of the French sociologist Pierre Bourdieu (1984) represents a long tradition of inquiry relating various expressions of cultural taste with social and family background. This has contributed to the debate about the hierarchical distribution of "cultural capital" (Bourdieu's concept) and the nature of mass (or popular) culture. In one respect, the lifestyle concept offers an escape from the presumption that media taste (unlike traditional aesthetic and artistic taste) is determined by social class and education, since lifestyles are, to some extent, self-chosen patterns of behavior and media use.

In commercial marketing research the lifestyle concept is helpful for classifying consumers into various types in ways that assist the targeting and design of advertising. For such purposes it is desirable to go beyond basic social-demographic categories and to make finer distinctions, especially with psychological dimensions. Lifestyle research developed out of ideas about social or psychological types, for instance Riesman, Glazer, and Denny's (1950) theory of inner- or outer-directed personalities and Maslow's (1968) theory of basic needs. A prominent example is Mitchell's (1983) delineation of nine American lifestyles, of which the three most significant types were: Belongers, Emulators, and Achievers. A related kind of typology that emerged from a study of the social and psychological origins of media use, with particular reference to social and community activism (Donohew et al., 1987), identified four types as: Disengaged Homemakers, Outgoing Activists, Restrained Activists, and Working-Class Climbers. This classification distinguished relevant aspects of media use according to a pattern of attitudes and beliefs. It also showed important gender differences.

Lifestyle research involves studying a wide range of social positional variables, behaviors (including media use and other leisure and consumption practices) and attitudes, tastes, and values. There is in fact no limit to the potential scope of such research nor, perhaps, to the number of media-relevant "lifestyles" that can be identified. It is also often possible to choose alternative ways of describing the same research findings, for instance by emphasizing different causal factors. These can be social (e.g., class and income) or cultural, or psychological and attitudinal.

These comments illustrate the weakness of the lifestyle concept. A lifestyle is in the end no more than a construct of theory or research that posits, or claims to discover, connections among several out of a vast array of potentially relevant variables. Any factor analysis of sufficient population data of the kind mentioned is likely to identify potential candidates for description as lifestyles. An extensive Swedish inquiry into youth and media use (Johansson & Miegel, 1992; Reimer, 1994) illustrates some of the benefits and also limitations of media lifestyle research. The findings show that media tastes and choices do contribute to a certain segmentation of everyday life and leisure patterns that can be called lifestyles and also, in turn, that what we might call a lifestyle can influence media use. But it also seems as if age, social class, and gender on their own account for much of the differentiation found.

One of the main problems with the concept is finding an appropriate level of analysis. Johansson and Miegel (1992) distinguish three levels: that of the whole society (for international comparisons), that of differences within societies and cultures, and, finally, the individual level. Of the latter they say the "lifestyles are expressions of individuals' ambitions to create their own specific, personal, social and cultural identities" (p. 23). The second level is the most commonly applied, often with rather confusing results. At the third level there are potentially as many lifestyles as there are individuals. Nevertheless, the concept is helpful in understanding the many different ways in which media are meaningfully interrelated with social and cultural experience.

Ethnicity and Media Use

A source of social differentiation that may be increasing in importance in modern urban living is associated with race and ethnicity. In some countries, there is a separate media provision for linguistic and ethnic minorities (Frachon & Vargaftig, 1995), and elsewhere there is often evidence of differential attention to mainstream media by minority members (see Becker,

Kosicki, & Jones, 1992; Real, 1989; Wilson & Gutiérrez, 1985). With respect to music, there are a variety of "black" and "white" styles and many other hybrid versions forged out of ethnic and cultural mixing (Lull, 1992). In this terrain, media use can be understood as an appropriate means of expression and enjoyment, as a shared exclusive experience, and as an identification with a certain kind of culture. Often, ethnic differences are more pronounced in interpretations and attitudes than in actual media choice behavior (Gray, 1992).

These aspects of audiencehood are very evident with respect to popular music, which has a very differentiated cultural production and which can respond to small differences and shifts of taste (Frith & Goodwin, 1990; Negus, 1992). While members of ethnic minorities are attracted to dominant media and to "mainstream" cultural taste for the same reasons as everyone else, there is also a place for the expression of minority cultural forms. These help to provide a more secure, valued, and familiar symbolic environment. Ethnic group identity (especially for black minorities in white society) has found support in distinctive cultural tastes. For instance, rap and hip-hop styles of music are at the center of complex social identities in several countries with sizeable black minorities (Lull, 1992).

Gendered Audiences

The idea that media use is notably and persistently "gendered" has also been developed in reception research, under the influence of feminist theory (Seiter et al., 1989). The differentiation of media use according to sex has long been recognized, and certain types of media are specifically produced for female audiences, often by women, especially perhaps certain magazines (Ferguson, 1983) and types of fiction (e.g., romance). Male audiences are also served by distinctive media types and genres.

What is new is a greater curiosity about the meaning of these differences and a search for an understanding of how the social construction of gender also influences media choice and vice versa. In this search, the methods of ethnography and depth research have been employed. Typically, the notion of an "interpretative community," as shaped by gender experience, plays a key part (Hermes, 1995). Audience research has often accompanied (perhaps followed) analyses of content that have also probed the "gendering" of media texts. In fact, it is hard to separate out audience- from content- and production-research.

Gendered audience experience is a complex outcome of a certain kind of media content, typical everyday routines, and the wider structure of what may still be described as "patriarchal society"—or a "man's world" as far as power is concerned. A much-cited example is Radway's (1984) research into one set of devoted (really addicted) women readers of mass produced romance fiction. Radway set out to account for the compulsive appeal of romance fiction by accepting in the first instance the main explanations offered by women readers themselves. From this perspective, romances offer an escape specifically designed for women, first of all by way of the act of reading, which establishes a private "space" and time, protected from incursion by husbands and family duties; second, by offering versions, albeit in fantasy form, of the ideal romance, which can be emotionally nurturing. Radway's evidence suggested that alternatives and images found by women readers in their fiction were at least mildly empowering and supportive, notwithstanding the tendency of critical feminism to view romance fiction as delusory and reactionary in tendency.

The notion of gendered audience has also been invoked in relation to another genre that attracts a largely female audience—that of radio and television "soap operas." There are several varieties of the species, but the early (American) version was broadcast on radio during the daytime to address an audience of women at home. Early studies of the genre (e.g., Herzog, 1953; Warner & Henry, 1948) pointed to the especial appeal of soap operas for women as housewives and mothers—not only because of their convenient scheduling but also through their content, which was a mixture of drama, advice, morality, fantasy, and symbolic support for the role of women at home.

More recent studies of television soap operas (e.g., Allen, 1989; Geraghty, 1991; Hobson, 1982, 1989) have linked their narrative form (continuity, indeterminacy) to typical features of the housewife's daily routine, which is fragmented and distracted (preventing continuous attention) but also flexible. Soap operas in general are significantly more preferred and watched by women, even when they recognize the low status of the genre (e.g., Alasuutari, 1992). Ethnographic research into female soap opera viewers indicates that the genre is widely appropriated as especially meant for women and often serves for conversation and reflection about viewers' own everyday experiences (Livingstone, 1988).

With respect to the audience for women's magazines, Hermes (1995) has identified a set of interpretative "repertoires" or structures of meaning in terms of which women readers account for their reading behavior and their relative attraction to the different varieties of the genre (ranging from feminist to traditional publications). Repertoires refer, for instance, to the sense of duty to support the cause of women or the mild guilt at reading traditional women's magazines. These sets of ideas are often mutually inconsistent or in dialogue with each other, but contradictions are made easier to handle by the relative lack of significance attached to the magazine medium by even their most faithful readers.

This typically detached attitude on the part of an audience, reflecting a widely understood gap between real-life experience and the media world, is, presumably, quite common. Ang's (1985) study of women fans of the television series *Dallas* (a special "glossy" type of soap opera) showed how common it is for enjoyment of fictional nonsense to be reconcilable with criticism of much of the content. Viewers can easily adopt an amused or ironic stance. It would be quite mistaken to define an audience according to any externally formed view (or any single view) of the content or medium in question. Audiences exist and pleasure is taken, independently of the specific content chosen and the criticism that it may attract on aesthetic, moral, or political grounds. Of course, the same applies to other genres and other audiences.

The essence of a gendered audience is not the sex ratio of its composition, but the degree to which conscious membership of an audience (audiencehood) is given some distinct meaning in terms of specific female or male experience. There are numerous indications in research into media use that gendered differences are associated with different preferences and satisfactions. For instance, Anderson, Collins, Schmitt, and Jacobovitz (1996) found that stressed women watched more game and variety shows, while stressed men watched more action and violent programming, thus accentuating differences that show up in the general audience. This is not to suggest that most mass media experience can be accounted for in gender terms, since there is much evidence of shared purpose and understanding across gender lines.

Another aspect of audience gendering is the degree to which the complex social act of using a domestic medium such as television is influenced by relations between the sexes and by particular sex roles. The classic exploration is probably that of Morley (1986), whose ethnographic study of family viewing emphasized the many unwritten rules, understandings, and patterns of behavior that develop in the micro-audience environment of even one family. Typically, the power to control (evening) viewing was exercised by the man (see also Lull, 1982a).

Women, in general, were found less likely to plan viewing or to watch continuously. They were more likely to do other things while viewing, to give way to the preferences of other family members for social reasons, to talk while viewing, to feel guilty for viewing alone. Women would be inclined to treat television as a resource for easing family tensions, reconciling quarrels, encouraging varying degrees of privacy or sociability in a viewing situation. Morley (1986) cites the example of men using their power of control to "get even" with their wives in some dispute, for instance by watching sports exclusively. Presumably women do something similar in return, when they get the chance. Finally, there is now an expanding field of research addressed to the influence of gender on the acquisition and use of new communication technologies in the home (Frissen, 1992; Moores, 1993).

Sociability and Social Uses of the Media

Mainstream communication science implicitly sets "media use" apart as a distinct and alternative type of behavior, one that necessarily displaces other activities. This way of thinking led early critics to bemoan the supposed "isolation" of the cinema spectator, the killing of conversation by radio and television, the decline of outdoor social life, and the retreat into family circles (privatization). More recent objects of critical attention in this vein are the Walkman-listening zombie and the young addict of computer games or the Internet who loses touch with reality.

There are obviously many individuals who are both socially isolated and also strongly addicted to media use behaviors that might reinforce their isolation. However, there is no decisive evidence of any general decline in social contact as a direct result of mass media use. An understandable concern about addiction to media has diverted attention from the more typical meanings of media attractiveness. Most uses of the media have been effectively rendered sociable. Media use is itself a ubiquitous form of normal social behavior and an acceptable substitute for actual social interaction. It is also widely perceived as a significant "agent of socialization"—an occasion for social learning and a means toward participation in the wider society (Rosengren & Windahl, 1989).

The sociability of the audience experience is evidenced by the following familiar (and well-attested) features of normal media use. We often share the experience of attending to the media with others, especially in the case of film and television; the media (e.g., television or music) are used to entertain other people or to ease social interaction; attending to the media is often accompanied by talk about the ongoing experience; the content of media (news items, stories, performances) provides an object of shared attention for many as well as topics of conversation. Media-related talk is especially useful in providing a nonintrusive basis of contact with strangers. Media in the home are frequently a background to virtually every other kind of activity, without necessarily impeding or displacing these activities. Kubey and Csikszentmihalyi (1991) for instance, reported that "63.5% of the time television was being viewed, people reported doing something else as well" (p. 75).

There is no clear evidence that the classic forms of interpersonal "sociability," such as conversation and "hanging out," have disappeared, although it is very likely that some domestic entertainments that were sociable, like card-playing, musical parties, and family games, have declined (although for other reasons as well). Rosengren and Windahl (1989), in their overview of findings of the long-term Swedish Media Panel research into child development, have found much evidence of varied and complex patterns linking media use with other social activities. They find "on the whole positive relations between children's television viewing and their social interaction" (p. 200). Age (grade in school), gender, and social class all played a part in mediating the link.

The relationships involved are different for books, television, and popular music. The following is one example from many found in this research. For middle-class boys in Grade 7 (age 13), television use offers "a route from home and parents to peers and dances. For those who use it a lot in Grade 9 (age 15) it seems to be a link to home, parents and school" (p. 203). As a socializing agent, the role of television appears to have been reversed over the span of 2 years' development. The fact that this is a long-term panel study makes the findings especially dependable.

It appears that the patterns of everyday socializing are both complex and changing as a result of new means of passing time. Most media use can be as sociable or not as one chooses, depending on our real-life resources (in terms of money, mobility, available friends, and social contacts). This is what

Rosengren and Windahl (1972) termed "interaction potential." In providing a substitute for real-life social contact, which might simply not be available, especially in modern urban living, the media often help to alleviate loneliness and stress caused by isolation.

Mass mediated social contact can supplement and complement as well as displace real personal contacts with others. As a result, the potential for social interaction can as well be enlarged by mass media as reduced. Evidence of a causal relation between social isolation and media use is hard to come by (see Canary & Spitzberg, 1993; Finn & Gomm, 1988; Perse & Rubin, 1990; Rubin, Perse, & Powell, 1989). Insofar as there is a general empirical answer to the question of relationship between social interaction and media use it seems that higher levels of "real" social contact are often accompanied by above average levels of contact with the media. This finding does not settle the issue, but the correlation can be understood as supporting the claim that being in an audience is most correctly to be defined as "social" rather than "nonsocial."

There are a variety of ways in which media use becomes intertwined with everyday life, especially in the case of television, which is such a ubiquitous accompaniment to domesticity. James Lull (1982a) has suggested a typology of social uses of television based on participant observation of families. Some of the points also apply to other media. The first type is referred to as *structural* and identifies the numerous ways in which the media provide a time frame for daily activities, beginning with an early news bulletin, an accompaniment to breakfast, and continuing, according to the daily schedule, to mark breaks from work, mealtimes, the return from work, and evening relaxation with familiar and suitable programming on radio and television. This is what Mendelsohn (1964) referred to as the function of radio in "bracketing the day." A media-derived structure of this kind provides a sense of companionship and marks off phases of the day, helping to establish appropriate moods. A second type is called *relational* and covers the points made earlier about content as a conversational "coin of exchange" and a way of easing social contacts of an informal but not intimate kind.

The third category is summarized in terms of *affiliation and avoidance,* referring to the fluctuating dynamics of social relations in which people want to be, by turns, socially close to, or separate from, others with whom they share the same physical space. Different media offer different opportunities for one or the other option. Affiliation is expressed by joining in the same spectatorship (e.g., a football game on TV) in varying degrees of participativeness.

Avoidance takes more diverse forms. Some involve the use of particular media that are by definition solitary in use, like books or headphone music. In public as well as private places, reading newspapers often expresses a wish to be left alone. Having separate television and radio receivers in different parts of a house helps in the dispersal of members of a household. These social devices are usually understood and accepted as legitimate, thus avoiding offence to others. It is impossible to separate out the more "legitimate" media use motive from the less acceptable aspect of self-isolation. In families, as children grow up, there is a fairly clear pattern of increasing dispersal of individual activities, which is closely related to the use of different media (von Feilitzen, 1976).

Of the remaining social uses named by Lull, one—*social learning*— covers a wide range of socializing aspects of media use (e.g., adopting certain role models), and a fifth carries the label *competence/dominance*. This refers to the socially structured power to control media use in a household, ranging from a decision to choose a daily newspaper to the use of the TV remote control, and including decision making over the acquisition of media hardware and software. It also refers to uses made of media-derived information and expertise to play the role of opinion leader in social contacts with family and friends (Katz & Lazarsfeld, 1955). Ethnographic research in domestic settings makes it clear that media use is often governed by quite complex, usually unspoken, rules and understandings that vary from one family to another (see Morley, 1986).

Audience Reception and the Negotiation of Meaning

The question of media effects lies outside the scope of this book, but it is important to draw attention, however briefly, to the wide implications of reception theory for the study of effects. New audience theory proposes that not only the significance of the media experience as such but also the meaning derived from media content is very dependent on the perceptions, experiences, and social location of audience members (Jensen, 1991). Audiences "decode" the meanings proposed by sources according to their own perspectives and wishes, although often within some shared framework of experience (Hall, 1980).

This certainly applies to the complex and ambiguous messages of fiction (e.g., the lessons drawn by women readers of pulp romance fiction—Radway, 1984). It is also true of the normative judgments about aesthetic or moral quality of media content, as discussed below. We cannot assume that even basic "factual" information will be understood as sent. The evidence for the seemingly poor or faulty understanding of news is overwhelming (e.g., Gunter, 1987; Robinson & Levy, 1986), although this is sometimes mistakenly attributed to deficiencies on the side of sender.

Reception analysis of news (e.g., Graber, 1984; Jensen, 1988) makes it clear that frameworks for understanding news depend very much on the social position and outlook of the receiver, who is both able and strongly inclined to fit the "facts" as reported into local and personal frames of interpretation and relevance. The audience for news is always busy constructing and developing cognitive and evaluative versions of "real" events in line with its own perspective on the world.

Media Use as Social Pathology

The various media have acquired a complex set of definitions that connect them to other aspects of personal social experience. On the one hand, they are an almost inevitable accompaniment to everyday life, requiring us to adapt our social habits (such as eating and conversation) to the fact of their existence. On the other hand, they are a valuable and varied resource for helping us to handle social situations and personal difficulties (Pearlin, 1959). With respect to the latter, we can think of media as a means of establishing a certain mood, of cheering us up, taking us out of ourselves, stimulating various feelings, helping us to remember and reflect as well forget. There is certainly evidence of media being consciously used for such purposes (Zillman & Bryant, 1985).

This discussion was introduced by casting doubt on the "desocializing" effect of media use, while admitting that abnormal degrees of self-isolation via the media do sometimes occur. It is impossible to draw a line between what is unusual or extreme and what is, in some sense, pathological or harmful. The same evidence can also be interpreted in different ways. Thus early studies of media "addiction" by children (e.g., Maccoby, 1954) found the more likely cause of "excessive" media use to be in family dislocation and other personal problems. Media use is often a compensation for social and psychological deprivations.

Overdependence on television was early on identified as potentially harmful for children (Himmelweit et al., 1958) or as a symptom of personal failure to develop or to adjust to reality. It was also, more simply, something perceived as of little value that got in the way of things that children, in particular, were thought better off doing (like playing games, going out, or doing homework). There was evidence to suggest that high use of television was indeed correlated with poor social adjustment by children (e.g., Halloran, Brown, & Chaney, 1970; Horton & Wohl, 1956; Maccoby, 1954; McLeod, Ward, & Tancill, 1965; Noble, 1975; Pearlin, 1959). For adults, heavy use of television and other media was associated empirically with other indicators of social marginality, especially sickness, old age, unemployment, and poverty (Smith, 1986). Despite these observations, there are reasons for rejecting the term *addiction,* with its associations of drug dependence. Finn (1992) examined various media use models and concluded that "data failed to support any conceptualization of excessive television viewing as a disease or . . . medical problem" (p. 422).

Some evidence does point to degrees of audience involvement with real or fictional media personalities that seems to verge on the irrational, even if not the pathological. There is plenty of somewhat anecdotal, though credible, evidence to show that individual audience members do develop strong personal attachments to fictional characters, for instance in long-running TV serials, to the extent that they mourn their fictional "deaths" and share emotionally in their joys. It is usually very difficult to assess just how deep such attachments really are. Lombard (1995) concluded from her research that "a variety of responses to television correspond with responses to unmediated experience . . . [to the extent that] audio-visual media are capable of blurring the distinction for media consumers between mediated symbolic and artificial experiences and non-mediated or 'real' experiences."

Normative Framing of Media Use

The preceding discussion is a reminder of the extent to which research into the media audience has taken place within a normative, even judgmental, framework (see Barwise & Ehrenberg, 1988, pp. 138ff.), itself a sign that media use has been thoroughly incorporated in the socialization process. Although, as we have seen, high media use does not in itself have to be viewed as harmful, the most basic norm applied to the media has been that you can have too much, even of a good thing. The normative framing of media use seems at first to run counter to the view that media use is a voluntary, free-time, "out-of-role," and generally pleasurable activity, more or less unrelated to any social obligation. Yet audience research continually uncovers the existence of value systems that informally serve to regulate media behavior. As Krcmar (1996) observes, "families have as many rules and disagreements about TV viewing as they do about such diverse topics as homework, eating habits and religious obligations" (p. 251). It is from the imposition of norms for media use in family contexts (with reference to parental responsibility) that we are most aware of normative control of media (Brown & Linne, 1976; Geiger & Sokol, 1959; Hedinsson, 1981; Rosengren & Windahl, 1989).

It is easy to lose sight of the extent to which we are socialized into routine audience behavior of all kinds and unconsciously learn rules and expectations concerning media. These are so extensive and can vary so much with time, place, and culture that they defy any exposition. Usually we are only aware of the rules when they are unexpectedly broken by other audience members or by the media themselves. For instance, a study by Nord (1995) of early Chicago newspapers uses letters from readers to demonstrate that they had a well-developed sense of what journalistic objectivity and editorial responsibility entailed. This showed up when they felt their newspaper had betrayed them by being biased, propagandistic, or by straying from familiar political positions. Many of the unwritten "rules" that we learn are built into familiar categories of media genres as well as into associations with particular channels and sources.

There is extensive evidence that the media are widely regarded by their own audiences as potentially influential for good or ill and thus in need of need of direction and control by society. At the very least, they should be supervised by parents. For instance, Gunter and Winstone (1993) report that 90% of a British sample think parents should discourage their children from watching too much TV, and large majorities support control over viewing in general. In the same survey, about 50% thought British television was strongly regulated, and 75% were satisfied with this or wanted even more control than was exercised at present.

There is also evidence that public opinion in several countries favors quite strong regulation for a range of media, including print, on a variety of grounds (see Golding & Van Snippenburg, 1995). Audiences are broadly concerned about media standards and feel that maintaining these standards can often require intervention. Public opinion does not generally allocate as much freedom to media as the media often claim for themselves.

While no doubt much of the normative concern about media stems from fears of unwanted influences, media use in itself can be regarded as morally dubious (as noted above). For instance, Steiner (1963) found a tendency for viewers to show guilt over their own high levels of television use, which he attributed to a legacy from the Protestant ethic, which frowns on "unproductive" uses of time. Among middle-class audiences, especially, a sensitivity to this value persists. Radway (1984) found similar kinds of guilt feelings among keen female readers of romantic fiction and for similar reasons: "guilt is the understandable result of their socialization within a culture that continues to value work above leisure and play" (p. 105). In both examples, guilt was more evidenced in words than in behavior, reflecting the influence of social desirability.

In her study of readers of women's magazines, Hermes (1995) found that within the "interpretative repertoires" (ideas that frame reading experiences) of women readers there was a place both for feelings of duty to read a feminist publication and guilt at enjoying traditional women's magazines. Barwise and Ehrenberg (1988) and Kubey and Csikszentmihalyi (1991) suggest that such guilt feelings (in relation to television) are typically quite weak (Hermes would probably agree with respect to magazines), but their persistence and ubiquity is, nevertheless, striking, in a supposedly hedonistic age and about such a harmless pleasure.

Norms for Content

Normative expectations relate not only to media use behavior, but also to aspects of media content. People voice complaints about, as well as appreciation of, the media. Positive response usually outweighs criticism, but what is striking is the fact that the performance of the media is so widely regarded as a proper topic for the expression of public attitudes, judgments, and opinions.

Audiences expect media to conform to certain norms of good taste and morality, sometimes also to other values, such as those of the local community, patriotism, and democracy. Norms for what is appropriate in fiction and entertainment usually refer to bad language, violence, sex, and the models of behavior offered by media. Here family life, the protection of children, and the personal susceptibilities and moral standards of adults are the main points of reference.

Morals aside, it is notable also that audiences are sensitive to the quality of media on grounds of political bias and fairness, often placing more emphasis on impartiality and reliability than on the media's own rights to freedom of expression (e.g., Comstock, 1988; Gunter & Winstone, 1993). Audiences can often seem intolerant of the public expression in the mainstream media of extreme or deviant political views. The norms applied by the audience to media information commonly refer to completeness and accuracy, balance, and diversity of opinion. News sources are often judged according to their relative credibility (Gaziano & McGrath, 1987).

Despite the evidence of a critical public attitude, rather few people seem personally offended by the media and actual use behavior shows a state of relative normlessness (see, e.g., Gunter & Winstone, 1993). This paradox may reflect the existence of private norms based on personal taste and preferences that, as with many aspects of behavior, do not correspond with the public norm. It also suggests that evaluative attitudes expressed toward media are somewhat superficial and learned as socially desirable rather than deeply internalized. This is not to say that personal preferences in choosing and responding to media content will not be influenced by an individual's own personal values (see Johansson & Miegel, 1992). Rather, these value influences are often implicit and beneath the surface.

Values applied to content often involve fine distinctions between one medium and another and one genre and another. For example, Alasuutari (1992) showed that Finnish television viewers deployed a sort of "moral hierarchy," according to which news and information were highly regarded and soap operas were seen as a "low" form of content, even by fans of soap operas (this perception is quite widespread; see, e.g., Ang, 1985; Morley, 1986; Seiter et al., 1989). They were expressing a consensus of judgment that they were aware of, without feeling personally bound to follow it. The nature of the hierarchy is not very surprising, since it reflects traditional cultural values and tastes, especially a respect for reality and information.

In line with other research findings, this "moral hierarchy" turns out to be more a question of attitude than of behavior, since favorite viewing patterns did not follow the normative prescription. There is plenty of evidence that audiences can and do distinguish between what they regard as the objective "quality" of content and their own personal preferences (likes and dislikes), which may deviate from these standards (Leggatt, 1991). One explanation, aside from simple inconsistency or failure to be as good as one would like, lies in the intrinsic satisfaction of watching *television* (the same would apply to reading), quite apart from the moral or aesthetic quality of content.

The relationship between audiences and their media experience is often far from simple and involves several dimensions of attitude and relationship. For instance, in their work on cultural differences among audiences in response to *Dallas,* Liebes and Katz (1990) distinguish several degrees and kinds of critical distance. One difference is between the "referential" and the critical. The former turns on the degree to which audience members see story events as being convincing, true to life, or relevant to their own lives. The second tends to invoke more aesthetic kinds of judgment, with reference to the narrative and another qualities of the text (see also Bildereyst, 1991; Livingstone, 1988).

Other forms of critical distance include an objection to some aspects of content on moral or ideological grounds. In other words, it seems that "experienced" audience members (these kinds of data came from regular and articulate viewers) have a fairly extensive repertoire of positions they can take up with respect to particular media contents. Similar general conclusions about women's magazines were drawn by Hermes (1995), and the complexity of audience response does not seem limited by the relative lack of reader involvement or the acknowledged superficiality of the content concerned.

Conclusion

We can conclude this discussion by noting that media are typically viewed by their audiences within a complex framework of expectation and judgment that is derived ultimately from an appreciation both of the public and social character of the media and of their significance in everyday life and the personal pleasure that they can give. This framework of assessment may not be routinely activated or consciously articulated by the average audience member, but the prescriptions that arise concerning media and their contents are usually very familiar.

The social uses of media are so inextricably built into routine practices that we are rarely conscious of them. The values most frequently expressed about content often stem from conventional judgments embedded in the culture or handed down by way of the socializing institutions of education, family, and religion. To a certain extent they also reflect differences of social power exerted by way of the class system. Sometimes they reflect differences of age, gender, race, and other bases of social distinction (e.g., fashion, cosmopolitanism). The influence of our own personal values on media use and content choice is complex, implicit, and concealed, not easy for research to uncover. Taken together, the ideas and evidence presented in this chapter discredit the notion of the audience as a sitting "target" for media manipulation and influence. In almost every respect of media choice and use and in the significance attached to media by their audiences, we can see a strong, even determining, influence of social and situational factors.

SEVEN

Communicator-Audience Relations

Bridging the Gap

The relationship between sender and receiver is central to any consideration of the media audience concept. Unlike the case of face-to-face contact, mediated (and especially mass-mediated) communication always involves a spatial and social distance between the participants. The world of media production is typically far removed from the context of consumption. This distance has to be bridged in one way or another for communication processes to continue in a meaningful, effective, and satisfying manner.

In practice, such gaps are usually closed by a combination of organizational strategies, presentational devices, and a complex web of conventions and understandings that are shared between communicators and audiences. These understandings have grown up over time, and they define the legitimacy, normality, and boundaries of communicative content and contacts, indicating who should address whom, in what manner, and for what purpose. They render society-wide and cross-cultural communication essentially unproblematic for most people most of the time.

There are general models of mass media systems (e.g., that of Westley & MacLean, 1957) that portray the links between mass media senders and receivers as kept in balance by feedback of various kinds from audiences to media organizations and from audiences to the "original communicators" (or sources) in society (Singer, 1973). Such models presume a self-righting mechanism that, in an open society, is mainly sustained by the pressure on media to meet the content requirements of audiences, in a competitive market environment, within the limits set by law, culture, and custom. Mass communicators have to compete for attention and income, and the best evidence of what the audience wants is provided by their past choice behavior.

In addition to the market, there are other bases for the relationship between the media and their audiences, bearing in mind that most messages are not originated by the media themselves, but only carried on behalf of other sources and organizations. The "original communicators" include political parties, advertisers, lobbyists, businesses, social action groups, and government departments, not to mention all the artists, writers, and performers.

These communication roles normally bring with them definitions and perceptions of the intended audiences that reduce uncertainty.

Some kinds of professional media communicators, especially print journalists, operate according to well-established standards of ethics and of responsibility to society and audience. The various sets of rules and codes (see Belsey & Chadwick, 1992; Christians & Rotzell, 1991) help journalists to establish a working relationship with the otherwise unknown "client." Many broadcasting organizations are also governed by even more explicit responsibility requirements and mechanisms for ensuring public accountability.

We should also note the continued existence of media that are not primarily commercial or neutral carriers but that exist in order to express particular social, cultural, political, or religious ideas and views and to help bind followers and members more closely to the cause, whatever it may be. The relationship between such media and their audiences is usually clear and unambiguous.

In this chapter we focus especially on actual "communicators" (journalists, writers for the media, editors, producers, performers, etc.) who need to orientate themselves on a day-to-day basis to a largely unseen and unknown public "out there." One of the lessons of research into media organizations is that the personal needs for orientation that communicators experience are not sufficiently met by the decisions of management, the abstractions of audience ratings, the guidance of focus groups, professional codes, or by other institutionalized mechanisms for controlling the market and maintaining contacts with actual or potential audiences.

It is helpful to envisage an attitude dimension on which media communicators tend to locate themselves with respect to the audience. This ranges from a very positive position of actively reaching out for contact, to a negative or defensive attitude toward the influence and demands of the audience. Location on this dimension can vary according to personal inclination as well as to the type of communicator role performed. Not uncommonly, media communicators find the audience threatening to their own performance, and for a variety of reasons. The more that communicators follow professional or personally chosen—rather than market-dictated—goals, the more potential for tension with the audience arises, since the market usually applies the predominant criterion of popularity.

The very diversity of a mass audience is often problematic for framing the message and choosing an appropriate form of address. Audience feedback in the form of low ratings can have arbitrary and harmful consequences, often unrelated to the "true" quality of performance, as perceived by communicators themselves. Research into media organizations suggests that many communicators see the mass audience as generally lacking the skills or qualifications to serve as adequate judges (e.g., Burns, 1969; Gans, 1979; Schlesinger, 1978). Media messages are usually put together and performance carried out under conditions of great pressure and effort, while the audience is perceived as relaxed, inattentive, and often unappreciative. Recurring problems of this kind are resolved in a variety of ways, but not always satisfactorily.

At the same time, the audience may also experience problems in its relations with communicators, however much is taken care of by the unwritten definitions of the situation, by information, and by the lessons of everyday experience. For most of the audience, the institutionalized forms of feedback, such as research and market forces, are unfamiliar and inadequate as a way of expressing views and feelings. More direct and personal forms of response require too much effort or are seen as ineffective. As members of audiences, most people find it difficult to articulate their demands and preferences. Nevertheless, we know that people in audiences do often have an active attitude to particular media, communicators, and messages. They can be highly engaged, and the degree of emotional involvement can approach that of normal human relationships.

The media could not operate efficiently without having developed their own mechanisms for handling the gap signaled here, quite apart from research and the evidence of market demand. There are a number of *gatekeeper* roles concerned with anticipating or expressing the interests and requirements of the audience. Gatekeepers can serve either side of the producer-consumer relationship and often both at the same time. Within news media, for instance, it is part of the editorial task to select and present according to criteria of relevance for the known audience. Book publishers and distributors do much the same all the time, as do film distributors and television channel controllers.

While less formally organized, the activities of reviewers and critics also serve the needs of the audience by providing advice and information. Usually these operate in the media and may have a self-interest that coincides with the interests of the media on which they comment, becoming incorporated into the market mechanism. Nevertheless, there are some independent critics and they do in general assist the audience, in practical ways, to negotiate problems of selection and ties of attachment to the communicators.

If we take a broader perspective, we can see that audience-communicator relationships are negotiated, managed, and defined within a larger institutional framework of relations between media and society. There are many different kinds of accountability that play a part, according to circumstances, extending much further than what is typically understood under the term *feedback*. For instance, as parents, citizens, members of minority groups or of political parties, we can seek to influence media and hold them to account for omissions or perceived failings.

Communicator Perspectives
on the Audience

Early research into the communicator-audience relationship drew on the theory of Herbert Mead (1934) and, before him, Charles Cooley (1908), especially by picking up the idea of an "imaginary interlocutor." The essence of the theory is that in order to communicate we need to have some known "reference person" or group to whom we can address ourselves, as well as having a shared cultural and social space and a common language. Where the other party to communication cannot be directly observed, it has to be constructed (or imagined). This involves a process of self-selection and stereotyping of the "significant other."

According to research by Bauer (1964a) and Pool and Shulman (1959), the reference groups that form the imagined targets of communication can influence the content of the message, as well as facilitate the process. Pool and Shulman wrote that it is the "audiences about whom the communicator thinks" (p. 148) that are important. In their study of news writing, it was found that journalists deployed an image of a reading public consisting of either supporters they chose to please or critics they liked to offend. Within such a framework, it became easier to write for an actual audience that was unknown. Subsequent research has often touched on the problem of anticipating and envisaging an audience, from the perspective of the communicator. While the insight just reported is often confirmed, we can find a number of different ways in which the nature of an audience is given substance and the distanced relationship made more manageable. The main devices for easing and mediating the relationship are described in the following sections.

The Audience as an Extension of the Communicator's Own Social World

Those who occupy the more autonomous and creative of mass communication production roles are likely to be the least yielding to some "target group" defined by audience research or imposed by management. The integrity of artistic creation does not really allow compromise of the highest standards, while editors and senior journalists expect freedom to report as they judge best, within the normal limits of their role in the organization. Nevertheless, they also need some conception of their audience, and a practical solution is to pay special attention to the reactions and views of personal contacts, friends, and relatives. This kind of reference group not only tends to mirror the communicator's own social and cultural milieu (Gans, 1979) but it is also likely to be supportive, rather than negative, in its response and of some practical use in putting the message together.

Among personal contacts, media people can also find not only their like-minded peers but occasional unthreatening representatives of less familiar social groups (e.g., the proverbial doorman, taxi-driver, cleaner, or office staff). Understandably, actual communicators prefer to receive feedback by word of mouth in familiar circumstances rather than in the form of authoritative and unchallengeable ratings.

Professional Reference Groups

It has commonly been found, especially in studies of journalists, that the most important reference group consists of colleagues. On matters governed by established standards of craft and profession, fellow professionals are likely to be recognized as the only competent judges (Burns, 1969; Tuchman, 1978; Tunstall, 1971). A key component of any claim to professionalism is usually the ability to judge the needs of clients (here, the audience) and to look after their interests better than they can themselves. In practice, the most immediate feedback is also likely to come from immediate colleagues. It has been noted that the media professional orientation is sometimes accompanied by a very negative attitude to the audience (Burns, 1969; Schlesinger, 1978). Burns (1969), writing about the attitude of BBC producers to their audience, observed that "service occupations . . . tend to carry with them a countervailing and ordinarily concealed posture of invidious hostility" (p. 55) to their clientele. The audience was often regarded as both fickle and unskilled, unable to recognize the intrinsic merits of work that is above their intellectual or aesthetic level.

In television, low audience ratings and other market failures can be explained by such deficiencies, rather than by low "quality" of the work or performance in question. In any case, the pursuit of professionalism also provides practical guidance and some insulation against the hard knocks of the competitive audience market on the one hand, and the crassness of management, on the other. It is also relevant to note that where professionals disagree with each other or with the organization, the audience (thus ratings and sales) is likely to be the final arbiter (Tunstall, 1971). In the end, what pleases the audience is the one objective criterion of success that cannot be ignored. It is also true that an ability to please the audience is a significant professional skill and goal in itself (Cantor, 1971). In highly competitive media market situations, it may be the single most important criterion of "quality."

Organizational Definition of Goals

More often than not, it is the media organization rather than the profession that provides orientation and guidance for relations with the audience. Tunstall (1971) distinguished newspaper organizational goals according to the kind of revenue sought for—especially as between advertising revenue and audience (sales and box-office) revenue. In the first case, the main requirement is to draw the attention of the *right* audience to the right message (the ad). In the second case, the main criterion of success is simply the size of the paying audience, regardless of who is reached.

However, Tunstall also notes the existence of "nonrevenue" goals. For instance, some media have a chosen task or mission that does not necessarily include great commercial success or high ratings in a mass market. The desire for political and social influence is quite a common ambition of media owners and editors. In such cases, the target audience and the desirable form of message receive specific definitions that reduce communicator uncertainty. This applies to noncommercial media, such as party political newspapers, and to public broadcasting, which usually has nonprofit social and cultural goals.

For instance, in the traditional European public broadcasting organization, such as the BBC, communicators have been required to "aim high," to maintain standards of integrity and cultural quality, whether rewarded by audience attention or not (Burns, 1969). The leadership of such organizations formulates appropriate goals with little reference to audience demands, although usually in accordance with an original charter or law. As a result of increased commercial competition the situation has now changed, but public broadcasting in Europe and elsewhere still has a mission that rises above the pursuit of ratings.

Somewhat similar remarks apply to the role in society of prestigious newspapers, like *Le Monde, The (London) Times,* and the *Washington Post,* which traditionally not only adopted high professional standards of journalism, but also chose some kind of political or societal goal beyond that required by the market; for instance, the wish to have political influence (Padioleau, 1985). Here, too, there has arisen a problem of reconciling professional and social goals with marketplace realities, and some commentators see a marked decline in standards of formerly elite media as a result of trying to follow popular demand (e.g., Bogart, 1995; Fallows, 1996). In the circumstances described, the communicator occupies a leadership role, inviting the audience to follow, but not compromising with laggards.

A variant of this situation arises wherever a medium has its own normative mission or purpose, whether political, cultural, or religious. Such media tend also to define their relationship with the audience as one of leadership and propagation of an ideology or ideal. Or they may simply try to express the voice of the group or public they serve. The audience will have a complementary view of their chosen media source. In these circumstances, the relationship between communicator and audience is likely to be more comfortable and balanced, supported by shared outlook and beliefs. Of course, there can be tensions, especially when either the beliefs or the supportive circumstances undergo change. Audiences can decline, and the media concerned can take a new, more commercial, course.

Product Image, Audience Stereotype

More typical of mainstream mass media is a situation in which media organizations and those who work within them develop certain stereotypes concerning the interests, expectations, and cultural tastes of their regular or intended audiences and seek to match these stereotypes with appropriate content. The aim is to maximize the correspondence between audience image and product image. This is part of a general process of responding to evidence of audience interests and building an appropriate market (Cantor, 1994; Ettema & Whitney, 1982; Ferguson & Perse, 1993; Martel & McCall, 1964; McDonald & Schechter, 1988). Experience teaches which media forms and contents have gone down best in the past, and the working assumption is that a slightly differentiated version of a successful format or basic product will work again next time. This applies to films, television shows, news stories, music (Negus, 1992; Ryan & Peterson, 1982). For the creative communicator, this often means leaving things to publicity managers and planners, who keep more closely in touch with the intended market.

The media often define their target audiences, as we have noted, in terms of lifestyle, partly to facilitate advertising. In so doing they tend to construct and offer to their audiences ready-made identities that go well beyond the choice of media messages alone. In earlier critical media theory this trend was viewed as manipulative and intrusive. C. Wright Mills (1956) wrote: "[the media] have provided us with new identities and new aspirations of what we should like to be, and what we should like to appear to be" (p. 314).

This way of handling the uncertainties of the audience can also be frustrating; it works against innovation, and it limits the communicator to a more passive role. It is also a source of tensions and conflicts for those who do have communicative purposes of their own or who want to work to the highest professional and craft standards (Cantor, 1971). On the other hand, it may also have some liberating potential for a communicator who happens to have discovered a personally successful formula, and it generally makes for greater security and continuity. It is probably a necessary condition for making money out of media production.

The Manipulation of Audience Participation

Under conditions of intensified competition for the audience, we can observe renewed efforts on the part of the media for actively controlling the relationship with the audience. It is not enough to set out wares for the passing customers, they have to be drawn into the bazaar and into personal engagement with media personalities and events. It becomes part of the communicator's aims and skills to accomplish this effect. The main goals are first to attract attention and then to promote feelings of personal involvement on the part of the audience.

There are different ways of trying to do this. In television, studio audiences play an increasingly frequent and prominent active role in a range of different formats, including game shows, talk shows, and public affairs programs. By drawing a representative section of the larger public into active involvement, the distance between presenters and other star performers and the audience at home is narrowed, and a sense of familiarity is encouraged (Livingstone & Lunt, 1994). The aim is to promote the "intimacy at a distance" (Horton & Wohl, 1956) that underlies the pseudo-personal ties formed with mass media personalities (see Chapter 6, under "Media Use as Social Pathology"). Some writers (e.g., Meyrowitz, 1986) suggest that the television camera can also be used so as to promote the desired form of parasocial relations.

The problem at issue here is not new, but goes to the heart of the debate over mass communication. Peters (1996) gives an account of how early radio communicators perceived and tried to solve the problem of "how to compensate for the missing bodies" (i.e., the face-to-face audience) 50 or 60 years ago. He describes three main approaches: first, discursive strategies, such as using "homey styles" and familiar forms of address; second, by promoting an imagined real audience by devices such as sound effects (canned laughter, applause) or telephone call-ins; third, by the simulation of personalized interaction on the air, with listeners encouraged to participate. All this gave rise to an impression of insincerity and a potential for distrust that led critical thinkers to accuse mass media of being fundamentally manipulative.

The style of "happy news" invented for American television in the 1970s and widely copied throughout the world exemplifies the same strategies applied in present-day television. The aim is to create an illusion of equality and closeness between powerful medium and distant audience and also to make the "bad news" brought by television less disturbing to the comfortable viewer at home. New technology increases the possibility for direct interactive formats that connect media presenters or performers, in a two-way link, with audiences at home. This can be done with increasing ease by way of the telephone or cable.

The View From the Audience

As has been remarked already, the audience does not generally experience its relations with the media and media communicators as problematic on a day-to-day basis. Under conditions of freedom and diversity, audiences choose their own media sources according to personal likes and perceptions of what is relevant and interesting. This need not entail either discomfort or uncertainty. Nevertheless, some effort is required on the part of the audience and some discomfort may be entailed, rather more than is commonly supposed. The first dimension to consider in audience-source relations is that of *affective direction*.

There are several potential sources of constraint, mostly of a mundane and routine character. First, although media are freely chosen by their audiences, actual people in audiences may not have personally chosen their media or the specific content to which they find themselves exposed. This applies where members of families, households, or other groups are subject to the choices of others about what is available to read, view, or listen to. Such media "micro-gatekeepers" may be parents, partners, friends, and others. It also applies where there are few or no real alternatives, for instance where there is only one city or local newspaper that is hard in practice to ignore.

There is usually a large flow of unrequested media messages by way of outdoor advertising, mail, telephone, and so on that gives rise to a similar situation. Even where we do choose our own media channel, source, and content, we can easily be dissatisfied with some aspects of media performance and there is much scope for negative responses to the media. We are continually faced with the need to select and evaluate, and this includes making choices *against* what we dislike.

Parasocial Relations

Apart from the existence of negative or positive feelings toward source, medium, or message, there is another relevant dimension of audience relationship to the media. This concerns the degree of *involvement* or attachment, which can vary from that of casual spectatorship to a high sense of personal commitment to a media person or performance. Voluntary attention and routinely positive attitudes do not in themselves entail any emotional commitment, so this is an added element. As noted, the invocation of a personal response from the audience, the encouragement of pseudo-participation are strategies frequently pursued by the media. As a result, it may be difficult empirically to distinguish "real" attachment from "artificial" attachment.

The notion of "parasocial interaction" was introduced by Horton and Wohl (1956) to describe the phenomenon of displacement of a human interlocutor by a media character or personality, treating it by implication as less satisfactory than real social interaction. In some circumstances, however, it may be open to a benign explanation or may be impelled by lack of satisfying real social contact. Scales have been developed for the empirical measurement of the degree of Para Social Interaction (PSI) (Austen, 1992), defined by Rubin et al. (1989) as "the degree to which audience members feel they interact with their favorite TV news persona" (p. 250).

Noble (1975), drawing on a study of Irish children in care, refers to television as providing a "screen community with whom the viewer regularly talks and interacts" (p. 63). He identified different degrees of involvement with media personalities and characters. One version can be described as "recognition," where a viewer has a very positive attachment to a particular media figure but does not lose a sense of reality and the experience can contribute positively to the formation of one's own identity. Noble reported that: "these [TV] characters serve as something akin to a screen community with whom the viewer regularly talks and interacts . . . this serves for many as an extended kin grouping" (pp. 63-64). Against this, there is the phenomenon of "identification," which means putting oneself so deeply into a TV character that one feels the same emotions and loses contact with reality. This may result in a personal "identity loss" and undue dependency on the media.

Rosengren et al. (1989) have distinguished several different kinds of "television relations," proposing a fourfold typology that they derived from two main dimensions of audience relations with the media. One of these they call *interaction*—having the feeling of interacting with actors on the screen. The second is the variable of degree of *identification* (involvement with some media figure). The extreme case of attachment to media occurs when a high degree of interaction coincides with a high degree of identification.

This situation is described as one of "capture" and likely to work against establishing normal personal ties with others. However we choose to judge these different states, we should at least be aware of the many kinds and degrees of attachment that the audience experiences. The reverse condition, with low identification and low involvement, is labeled "detachment."

While the two factors of evaluative attitude and degree of emotional involvement are probably the most important variables to keep in mind, there are a number of other ways in which audiences are connected to "distant" media sources. The following are the most relevant mechanisms that help to guide media choice and evaluation and to resolve potential uncertainties.

Social Milieux and Peer Groups

Many routine and habitual contacts with media are rendered natural and unproblematic by their becoming an integral part of a familiar environment and set of practices. These are governed by ties with family, neighborhood, friends and associates at school, work, and more. Particular media, patterns of use, types of content, become associated with our own identity, often without conscious individual choice. In this way, our relations with the media are unobtrusively defined for us. Sometimes, there may be a conscious choice to strengthen an identification with others by adapting our own choice and use of media.

A feature of contemporary social life (although it is not strictly new) is the emergence of a variety of lifestyles (see Chapter 6, under "Lifestyle") that are composite sets of cultural choices and practices structured to a certain extent by material conditions of locality, environment, occupation, income, and social background. Reimer (1994) says that the concept "is intended to capture the specific cultural practices of each status group" (p. 61). A lifestyle is expressed through cultural and behavioral choices, especially through various forms of consumption, including mass media.

For most people, the adoption of a certain way of life, including its component of media and other symbolic goods, is a normal part of growing up and forming tastes, interests, and friendships. The same process can operate at a collective level. For instance, immigrants finding their way in a new country often share a common pattern of media use. They are faced in their new environment with pressures to adapt, to discover new ties with unfamiliar media, or to accept a degree of isolation. These circumstances often lead to a strengthening of ties with the media of the country of origin and an enhanced sense of identity. The same can apply to a more numerous kind of immigrant—those who move from country to city—for whom the mass media often play an enhanced role. In Europe, cable and satellite television services for immigrants have grown rapidly in countries with large migrant inflows, especially Germany, France, the United Kingdom, and The Netherlands (Frachon & Vargaftig, 1995; Gillespie, 1995). Television is picked up from North Africa, Turkey, and Pakistan. Before the satellite era, videos served the same purpose. Gillespie shows how television and video viewing has long been used to negotiate new identities and maintain old ones.

Media Fandom

Audience experience has always been characterized by occasions of greatly accentuated and specified attachment to particular performers (most especially), but also to certain kinds of performance (types of music, genres of film or fiction). The weakest kind of fandom is simply an attraction to a medium (as in the old expression "film fan"). The strongest version involves a high degree of emotional investment and activity centering on a media personality. Something rather similar, but less intense, can occur with followers of a particular television series, when attachment to a fictional character gets mixed up with attachment to the actor, or when the distinction between fiction and reality is lost sight of. Fandom is best considered as something collective—a consciously shared feeling of more or less intense attraction. There are individual fans, of course, but it would be hard to be a lone fan and the concept would be redundant. Fandom has always been promoted and stimulated by the media publicity arm for obvious reasons (see Sabal, 1992) and by numerous means (especially by additional media products that center on the star in question), but it is also generated by fans themselves, when they associate with each other and express their attachment in public ways (T-shirts, fanzines, style, etc.; see L. Lewis, 1992). According to recent cultural theory (e.g., Fiske, 1992), fandom involves an element of actual media "production" by the audience itself, since the activities of fans extend the media event.

By definition, fandom defines relations with the media in a satisfying way and bridges the inevitable real "distance" between star and stargazer. Nevertheless, it can also be a painful experience, involving high expectations and vicarious emotional attachments that make the fan potentially vulnerable. Presumably, any such "costs" incurred though fandom are not normally disproportionate to the satisfactions obtained, although in some cases a loss of contact with reality can go too far. Fandom can also have a downside for the object of affection, since fans can be fickle and unforgiving and will ultimately desert. They also treat stars as objects of gossip, envy, and dislike (Alberoni, 1972), often encouraged in this by other media.

Audience as Rational Consumers

True fandom shades into a much more routine phenomenon of forming and expressing media tastes and preferences, as noted above. This is just a normal response to the process of media production and distribution, which places a large number of differentiated media products on the market. The audience is a set of customers whose relation to the media source is much the same as in other consumer markets. They look for suitable products, value for money, standards of quality, and reliability. The study of audience "uses and gratifications" as described earlier, incorporates this notion (although not only this). A typical model of media choice, such as that of Palmgreen and Rayburn (1985), represents the process by which an audience member chooses on the basis of some expected satisfaction and responds according to actual experience (see Chapter 5, Figure 5.2).

In a rational consumer model of this kind, the relation with a source is essentially uninvolved and *calculative*. One media product can be substituted for another or one supplier for another supplier. Late 20th-century media, characterized by changes of ownership, many new channels and media products, lower loyalty, and so on, are presumably also characterized by weak and mainly functional ties of the kind described. Even so, consumers do also express clear and stable expectations, they learn from experience, and they develop product or brand loyalties. The difference between new and old media situations may not be so great as it appears at first sight.

Normative Ties Back to the Media

Complementary to the media "with a mission" as described above, are audiences that share with their chosen media a particular outlook or belief, whether based on politics, religion, or culture. While the decline of a specifically political and ideological press in modern society has often been noted, there are some counterindications. Politics has to some extent changed its character, as reflected in many different causes, issues, and movements that are represented in many new media channels and formats. For instance, the talk show, phone-in show, and audience participation show are taking over from traditional forms of political communication (Livingstone & Lunt, 1994). The cumulative audiences for politically involving media use can still be large, especially for things to do with the various social problems, the environment, human (and animal) rights, racial discrimination, and many other causes and issues. Religion also, in somewhat new forms (especially fundamentalist, inspirational, revivalist), has become a significant basis for new kinds of media attachment in some countries.

Normative frameworks of morals and belief (as we have noted above) still play quite a strong part in structuring attitudes to the media. Each country and culture tends to have its own particular taboos or sacred cows that media have to respect, ultimately because of public feelings. There are written and unwritten codes that govern what the media do and that reflect what influential sections of the general media public prefer. The reasons lie in beliefs about the important public role of the media and also in the privileged access that media have to the domestic, private, sphere. A perception of the power of the media to influence on many important matters also plays a part. The relevant standards are usually fairly consensual and they are shared between the public and those media that consider themselves responsible.

Forms of Accountability to the Audience

Even in a free media market, there are quite a few institutionalized mechanisms for linking media to their audiences, aside from research or the normal process of maintaining good consumer relations. The topic takes us into another territory—that of media accountability to society—but it is useful to be reminded of some more or less formal aspects of the media-audience relationship. These include: media regulations designed to protect the audience; various forms of public service broadcasting; codes of practice and ethics within media organizations; procedures for handling audience complaints; the activities of voluntary audience pressure and interest groups.

The field of media regulation is too large to survey here, but we should keep in mind that all countries have laws, regulations, and controls (including much industry self-regulation designed to fend off regulation) that reflect claims of the audience to certain rights and to protection (from the media). Regulations range widely and often cover the following matters in one way or another: advertising standards in matters of accuracy and good taste; the safeguarding of minors, especially in matters concerning sex and violence; concentration of media control and ownership; supporting educational and cultural objectives; the protection of minority rights, for instance those of ethnic groups. The "public interest" in this context is often synonymous with the "audience interest" (although not in the sense of what interests the audience).

Public service broadcasting, although mainly confined to countries with European regulatory traditions, typically involves a particular view of media responsibility to its audience. Broadcasting is defined as a nonprofit activity that should aim first to serve the public interest, not just by pleasing audiences but by meeting a broad range of communication needs and by contributing to the general welfare of the society. Most often, public broadcasting is financed from a levy on all audience members and is made accountable to the public through the democratic political process. Broad goals of service are set and accounts are regularly rendered to supervisory bodies and parliaments. Audience members respond as voters and citizens as well as viewers, listeners, and consumers (Avery, 1993). There are often a great variety of social organizations involved in the public accounting process and many ways of expressing audience wishes and views, varying from place to place (see Blumler & Mitchell, 1994). Many are voluntary, but are sometimes formalized into Advisory Councils, or procedures for expressing public opinion and handling specific complaints.

On the matter of audience complaints, there has been a general growth of institutional means for airing and hearing complaints about alleged offenses. The print media are normally less formally accountable than broadcasting, but are nevertheless often subject to public scrutiny and trial by opinion or political pressure. The main forms are those of press or newspaper councils, which typically invite and adjudicate on specific complaints from the public about media performance. Such bodies usually aim to represent the interests of the industry and profession as well as the public and, lacking legal powers, work mainly through the power of publicity. Similar functions may also be carried out by newspaper ombudsmen. In some countries, commissions of enquiry carry out periodic reviews of press structure and standards, following the lead given by the American Commission on Freedom of the Press in the 1940s (see Blanchard, 1977).

Responsibilities to audiences are recognized by many media professionals, and these are often expressed in codes of practice that govern a wide range of media content forms, especially news content (Belsey & Chadwick, 1992; Christians & Rotzell, 1991). Generally, such codes are policed by media organizations themselves as part of their own defence mechanisms against external criticism, but they do enshrine some important ideas about the relationship between communicator and audiences and the role of media in society. They usually promise truth and accuracy in news and responsibility on broader social issues.

Where formalized means of redress are lacking or weak, we often see pressure groups at work that claim to represent the interests of a section of the audience and that can be very active in giving publicity to perceived media failures and failings, both on particular cases and as a general tendency. Such bodies often speak out on behalf of particular social groups, like children, ethnic minorities, homosexuals, or women. They are not usually very representative of the general audience, but they can often be very effective beyond their size or social power (Montgomery, 1989), and their operations help to keep some check on the media.

Conclusion

This chapter has taken us a long way from the earliest notion of an audience as a more or less anonymous, socially isolated, and passive set of individuals at the receiving end of one-way impersonal communication. There hardly seems any validity in such a version of the "mass audience," however large the audience may be. The limited nature of direct interaction that is permitted by the technology and circumstances of traditional kinds of mass media does not prevent the emergence of an extensive and complex set of compensatory arrangements as well as numerous socially defined or personally imagined webs of relationships and role definitions (for audience members and communicators) that make up for seeming deficiencies.

In the light of this evidence, one may be led to wonder whether inserting the technology for potential response (interactive media) actually represents any kind of "revolution" at all. Such technologies are not needed in order to bring about an adequate mutual positioning and interrelationship of the interlocutors in the web of mass communication. When interactive technologies are fully in place, they will be largely subordinated to social practices and definitions of the kind that already exist.

EIGHT

The Audience in Flux

The End of the Audience?

The mass media audience continually changes, as new media are added to the spectrum of possibilities and old ones adapt. Before newspaper reading had reached its peak in North America and Europe, film and then radio began to offer alternatives to reading. In the 1960s, both cinema and radio audiences declined substantially in response to the new mass medium of television. None of the "pre-television" media can yet be considered defunct, yet we continually hear proclamations of a revolution that will sweep away much of the flora and fauna of the old media landscape, and along with it the audience as we used to know it.

The proclamation of the "end of the audience" is, as we have seen, also the outcome of new theory, a change in the way of conceptualizing the audience. This has involved a move away from the perspective of the sender to that of the receiver and also a recognition of the abstracted and artificially constructed character of audiences in the typical media industry discourse. New and different audiences can be constituted by people themselves based on some shared interest or identity. The "audience" is no longer unilaterally defined by media industries and sources, whether as a market or a public. The once clear distinction between sender and receiver, which is crucial to the old definition of audience, is no longer held to be valid.

As always, we have to look for causes of change in social circumstances as well as in media technology and structure. In the light of experience, we should be duly skeptical about claims of a communication revolution arising from technology (see Schement & Curtis, 1995), but fundamental shifts are under way. More and new kinds of audience are being added, and old patterns of media use are being challenged.

Technology as a Source of Change

The most immediate driving force, as always, is *technology,* although a genuine "communications revolution" requires more than just changes in the way messages are distributed or a shift in the distribution of audience attention time as between different media. The central point of the current "revolutionary" argument has to do with the decline and coming fall of the *mass* audience that, as we saw, really only came into being within the 20th century.

Technology is now (yet again) undermining the probability and necessity of the mass audience that was itself a product of several forces: urban concentration; technologies of relatively cheap mass dissemination (economies of scale); limited supplies of "software" (media content) and high costs of individual reception; social centralization (monopolism or statism); and nationalism. Even before television had reached its apex and before the new electronic media forms had taken shape, the "decline of mass media" was being proclaimed (Maisel, 1973). This view was based on clear evidence in publishing and other media of increasing differentiation and specialization, following initial saturation of the mass market. It is a trend common to other industries and may be regarded as the stimulus to the adoption of new technologies rather than as their consequence.

The dominant model of the mass communication process at mid-20th century, nationally and internationally, was center-peripheral in form, following what has been called an "allocutive" pattern—that of direct address from one to many (see Chapter 3 under "The Breakup of the Mass Audience: New Types Emerge"; see also Bordewijk & van Kaam, 1986). This model is gradually being supplemented or replaced by different patterns (so the argument goes). One is a "consultative" pattern, in which receivers seek out and choose what they want, when they want it, and from a wide range of informational and cultural offerings. The other main pattern is an "interactive" one, in which conversations and exchanges of information are possible between senders and receivers, without reference to a center, by way of an infinitely extensible network linking everyone.

The earliest means of mass communication were industrial technologies that enormously expanded the power of dissemination from a center, but that approached their maximum capacity for distribution without achieving great diversity and without engaging their audiences in *active* communication. They followed an industrial logic of production for a mass consumer market. They also clearly differentiated public and open communication from the private and personal sphere. The role implicitly assigned to the audience, as determined by technology, was predominantly that of passive, but attentive, spectator and consumer. Only small-scale media could claim to be at all interactive, and these were typically local, specialized, and slow.

The new technologies are electronic—fast, clean, reliable, expandable, flexible, and with low (and rapidly declining) unit message costs. In their latest, still emerging, forms we are promised a global network of electronic highways through cyberspace in which personal contact with distant others can be combined with enormous choice of access to software and data of all kinds. The distinction between public and private communication is no longer supported by the technology, because of convergence of means of distribution and of the functions that they serve.

The typical audience role can cease to be that of passive listener, consumer, receiver, or target. Instead it will encompass any of the following: seeker; consultant; browser; respondent; interlocutor; or conversationalist. Certainly a change of this kind, after a century of the rise of the mass audience, could indeed be called revolutionary.

The history of media technologies (Marvin, 1988; Winston, 1986) offers plentiful evidence of the tendency for proponents of a new technology to offer, along with the hardware, a model of the way in which it might or should be used. This has certainly applied to the telephone, radio, television, and the personal computer. According to Bandini (1995), we can say that audiences are constructed initially by the inventors of technology. However, the subsequent history of media also demonstrates that the users eventually "reinvent" technology (Rice & Rogers, 1980).

Social and Economic Forces

In the past 20 years or so, while the new possibilities have been emerging, there have been other changes that have reinforced the influence of technology. These include rapid economic growth, greater productivity, and the opening up of new consumer societies, especially in the Far East. The spread of liberal economic doctrines (leading to media deregulation) and the decline of communism have contributed to the process. Between them, they have encouraged individualism (privatization) and secularization. Older mass organizations, such as trade unions and political parties, have also declined. Centralized public monopolies are in retreat. The increasing wealth and disposable income in countries most penetrated by mass media have encouraged diversification of products and of markets. Population growth has slowed or stopped and big cities are shrinking. All forms of mobility are on the increase and telephony connects more and more people. The social preconditions for the formation of mass audiences are now generally in decline in the more advanced industrial societies.

Another relevant force for change in which we can discern both communicative causes and also effects for communication is the *internationalization* (globalization) of practically everything. The world has seemed to shrink, because of faster physical travel and instantaneous transglobal communication, as well as because of reduced political and trade barriers. Obstacles of time and space are overcome (Ferguson, 1992). The greater sharing of cultural forms and practices leads to more shared experience. The Occident and Orient approach and become acquainted with each other, driven primarily by economic motives and necessities. The nation-state is in relative decline as transnational cooperation on many things becomes more important than sovereignty for its own sake. Effective global political institutions are seen to be more necessary than ever.

This summary of factors influential in audience change would be incomplete without reference to media *market forces*. The rise and rise of the media as business and industry is readily observable. Within a wider context of developments that make information increasingly central to society, the mass media are seen as one of the main economic growth points. There is a steady and growing demand for media products and services as economic growth produces surplus consumer income and free time. The United States is unusual in having entertainment as its second largest export industry, but the fact is symptomatic of broader changes in patterns of trade.

The Impact on Audiences

The implications for the audience include: more and more pressure to consume and a tendency to be served by larger and larger media firms. More significant perhaps, the meaning of the concept of audience as market is reinforced and extended, especially in the sense of a market for new domestic hardware. The audience consists of buyers and *users* of technology as much as of receivers of messages. The economic processes mentioned have mixed implications for the future of the audience. On the one hand, they encourage the growth of even larger audiences as a result of media concentration and because large audiences are good for cash flow and certain kinds of advertising. On the other hand, they create many new specialized audiences willing to pay high prices for new media products and channels. This somewhat contradictory state of affairs is an additional reason for caution in predicting the end of the old mass audience.

Such changes have big implications for the idea of an audience that, in its original form, was rather stable, confined within national boundaries, and clearly delineated by local and particular cultural tastes and means of expression. Media businesses used to be rather small, slow moving, and national in character. Two main kinds of change are involved and both are well under way One is a matter of capacity and volume—there are many more sources, more distributors, more media products, more means of distribution, more space on the channels, and all at steadily reducing real costs to the media consumer (the intended audience). The second change is qualitative and is represented by the computer-based interactive media (or quasi-interactive ones like teletext and CD-ROM). New technologies for recording, storage, and replay of all kinds of media increase the flexibility of media use and potentially free the audience from management and control by the media organization.

There is also a measure of *convergence* between the technologies used for public dissemination of messages and those (especially telecoms based) used for interpersonal (often intra- or interorganizational) communication.

There is a certain "personalization" (or just individualization) of public communication (e.g., individual access to electronic newspapers or audiotext) and "private" communication becomes more public, or at least more widely shared with strangers. This happens by way of the Internet or electronic eavesdropping, but also by phone and mail selling, advertising, and public information. As yet these trends are only just starting.

One of the impacts of media change that has long been envisaged and investigated has revolved around the notion of "overabundance" and information overload. The audience may be thought to experience problems as a result of the new media abundance, since it is being continually faced with additional choices and loses some familiar guidelines. There is no doubt that production and supply of information of all kinds (not only media) have been increasing at an exponential rate, outstripping the capacity of people to consume or use (Neuman & Pool, 1986). People have limited resources of time and money to give to the consumption of information, and it is quite obvious that audiences have not grown in extent in proportion to the possibilities for consumption. It is striking, for instance, that while Europe has experienced a several-fold increase in the supply of television programming in the past decade, the average amount of time spent viewing has barely increased.

One major response to this "overload," according to Neuman and Pool (1986), is a pro rata decline in the degree of attentiveness. They express this relation in terms of an equilibrium model that reflects the fact that the higher the level of media exposure, the lower the "quality" of attention. Only in this way can discomfort be avoided. It is a proposition that fits with evidence concerning individual television viewing. Kubey and Csikszentmihalyi (1991), for instance, found that "heavy" viewers were less alert and found the experience less rewarding.

An additional and paradoxical consequence of oversupply is that it increases the need on the part of audiences for the gatekeeping services that were traditionally supplied by the old media by way of their selecting, editing, packaging, and marketing activities. The supposed advantage of the new media in bypassing these "filters" can also be burdensome, and the more that gatekeeping and editing continue, the more audiences in the older sense will also survive.

Another common and plausible prediction about the effect of new technologies of communication on audiences (drawing more on qualitative than quantitative change) is that there will be a trend toward segmentation and fragmentation. This is a logical consequence of the great increase in opportunities for audiences to form, without any corresponding increase in numbers of media users or in the time available for media use (Webster, 1986). Formerly, audiences were predominantly recruited according to a geographical pattern of nation, region, city, and so on, with all residents sharing the same sources. Now they form according to factors that cut across residential patterns and have more to do with tastes and lifestyles.

Audiences are likely to become more internally homogeneous, because of greater specialization in media offerings (special interest periodicals, single-theme television or radio channels, local cable, etc.) and because of greater opportunities to choose specific types of content from the many new distributors. This is what is meant by *segmentation*. It is a process driven in part by the wish of media to create and manage new consumer markets and to deliver appropriate audiences to advertisers. There is clear evidence from the United States (and it is logical to assume a similar pattern elsewhere) that the homogeneity of audiences for television cable channels (measured according to standard demographics) is much higher than for national broadcast channels. Among the cable channels there is a considerable variation that tends to parallel the specificity of content and also correlate (negatively) with audience size (Barnes & Thomson, 1994, p. 89).

Fragmentation refers to the process whereby the same amount of audience attention is dispersed over more and more media sources. The search by individuals among new multimedia sources can theoretically lead to the ultimate degree of diversification and individualization, since all choices will be personal and unrelated in time and place to any other. This does appear to spell the end of the audience as a social collectivity—a formation with the possibility of a shared experience and sense of common belonging. Media users will have no more in common with each other (and no pattern of shared activity) than, say, car drivers or users of any other consumer product (although one should not underestimate the continuing collective and socially patterned character of "individual" consumption).

More Power to the Audience?

On the face of it, such trends also entail a shift of "power" to media consumers—putting the receiver more in charge and reducing the manipulative capacity of communication production and distribution organizations.

However, it also means that there is no longer any mechanism for exercising this new-found power on the "collective" behalf. The audience seems to have been transformed into a disparate set of consumers with no expressed common interest or institutionalized presence. People in audiences are in some respects more dependent on, and more vulnerable to, powerful media suppliers than before. They have no more power than consumers in any other market.

As Cantor (1994) comments, "Audiences-as-market-segments rather than audiences-as-cultural-politicians remain the most powerful influence on television content" (p. 168). But this aggregate (market) influence (see also McDonald & Schechter, 1988, and Ferguson & Perse, 1993) is far removed from that of public opinion or organized collective action and can easily be deflected, manipulated, and selectively interpreted by suppliers in the media market.

The multiplication of media and of means of distribution does also theoretically open the way for more diversity of "communicators" (primarily the organized media suppliers) and for more competition to please the audience, but this outcome is not guaranteed and, typically, the structure of media industries does not change as dramatically as the technology would permit. The same owners have remained largely in charge, although often swollen by takeovers, and their manner of operation is the same. Market forces, nationally as well as globally, seem to favor larger media conglomerates spreading across several different kinds of media (vertical and horizontal integration). For reasons of industrial policy, governments put fewer obstacles in the way of these monopolistic trends.

The earlier "mass audiences" for particular large-scale television channels or newspapers, for instance, did not have institutionalized rights, but their claims could be heard and they sometimes expressed themselves with the force of public opinion, which could not be completely disregarded. The media in question were often national in character, more politicized, and with something of the character of public institutions. The modern multimedia conglomerate, which may also be a transnational corporation, tends to avoid having any public presence except as required by market operations and has no particular responsibility or commitment to a national or local audience, beyond what is called for by good business practice.

A related aspect of the changes described here is a decline in the strength of ties that bind people to their chosen media sources. The "traditional" audience (as public) could and sometimes did maintain ties of loyalty (even affection or respect) to its chosen source, based on values shared with the medium and with fellow members of the audience. The loyalty of readers, listeners, and viewers was an important element of stability in the media system and contributed to the role that media played in society, as well as helping to secure the longer-term survival of media.

The new media users (customers/consumers) usually have no particular loyalty to their media suppliers, who are just agencies for making the connections personally chosen by individual consumers. There may be exceptions, for instance in the phenomenon of the community of Internet users, with a shared communication culture, but in general, the new situation promises to be one of greater individualism, self-interest, impersonality, and uncertainty and flux than in the past.

Less Power to the Media?

The fragmentation and segmentation of audiences has already made life more difficult for would-be persuaders, advertisers, and propagandists of varied kinds. It is simply harder, more expensive, and more unpredictable to reach any large general public, although smaller target groups may be easier to locate. The intended audience has more chance to escape exposure to unwanted sources and messages. If Neuman and Pool (1986) are correct, the audience is also less attentive to messages received than was the case in the early days of radio and television, as a result of more media channels seeking a near-constant amount of attention. They note, "Each item of information produced faces a more competitive market and, on average, a smaller and less attentive audience" (p. 74)

The changes described point also to a qualitative effect that reduces the likelihood of influence even when attention is given. The new media consumer typically has less time and motivation and has nothing invested in the relationship to incline him or her to respond. In effect, there ceases to be a social relationship between medium (communicator) and audience, although one may still flourish between individuals and particular performers or information sources "somewhere out there." There are certainly less likely to be normative ties between media and audiences of the kind described earlier, and this implies a lower degree of source influence on receiver opinion and belief.

The media themselves may not be so concerned about the reduced "quality" of the relationship with audiences, because the numbers are what matter most. However, for politicians, advertisers, pressure groups, campaigners, and advocates of all kinds who want to influence behavior and opinion, the emerging media situation does represent a potential problem. Much greater ingenuity is now required to catch attention and engage an audience.

The "Escape" of the Audience

The media are also affected by the seeming loss of control implied in audience fragmentation and dispersion. The title of Ien Ang's book *Desperately Seeking the Audience* (1991) sums up the plight of media institutions under new and more competitive conditions. The old form of organized and predictable delivery of audiences to the media made it relatively easy to keep track of audience size; composition; and patterns of demand, use, and satisfaction. The larger the audience, the easier it was to get accurate measurements by survey research. The audience of old was also relatively stable in composition and regular and predictable in its aggregate behavior. All this made for ease of planning, supplying, accounting for results, and selling audiences to advertisers. There is no less need, under the new conditions, to keep track of the audience, but it is more difficult and more expensive, despite improvements in the technology available for research.

According to Barnes and Thomson (1994), the well-established process of specialization in magazines was facilitated by improvements in computer analysis of audience survey data that enabled publishers to offer the right kind of market segment to advertisers in a convincing way. A similar process is now under way, with electronic audience measurement technologies spearheading the process of television audience specialization.

A wide range of media products (such as CDs, video recordings, books) can be tracked by way of computerized records of sales, supplemented by surveys. Use of television receivers can be monitored in great detail by electronic "people meters." Telephone use is also automatically registered. But there still remains a large and possibly increasing terrain of media use (especially where home computers are involved) where accurate and detailed information cannot easily be collected about what is going on.

If Barnes and Thomson (1994) are correct, however, the diversification of the distribution system, certainly in advertiser-supported media markets, cannot far outpace the capacity of technologies to track audiences. In light of this, it is interesting to note that in Europe, where advertiser support has always been relatively less important for all media than in the United States, the most commercially promising developments of cable and satellite channels have been in the form of subscription services, where audience tracking is assured.

The potential "escape" of the audience from agents of control and monitoring might be seen as a credit item on the side of audience power as against media power, although it is not clear that "the audience" actually benefits from its greater anonymity or unknowability. At least we can see some (probably welcome) limits to the power of media organizations to control by way of information. However, the media redouble their efforts by other means to keep their audiences on a leash, using intelligence gathering, propaganda, and publicity. One result, as we will see, is that the fragmentation and dispersal of audiences has so far only gone a limited way. We cannot assume that the new electronic media used privately in the home are less subject to surveillance than the old public media (Gandy, 1989).

Fragmentation: Varieties and Limits

We can sum up the discussion of audience fragmentation in terms of four succeeding stages as shown in Figure 8.1. This applies especially to television, which is at the center of the forces for change. In the early years of television (1950s and 1960s), most viewers in most countries had a limited choice of up to three central or national channels (the United States was better served). The same media experience was widely shared and quite homogeneous. This Unitary Model implies a single audience that is more or less coextensive with the general public. As supply of content and channels increases, there is more diversity and more distinctive options emerge within the framework of a unitary model (e.g., daytime and nighttime television, regional variations). This is a pattern of limited internal diversification and can be called a Pluralism Model. The third, a Core-Periphery Model, is one in which the multiplication of channels makes possible additional and competing alternatives outside this framework. It becomes possible to enjoy a television diet that differs significantly from the majority or mainstream. The final stage envisaged in Figure 8.1 is labeled as a Breakup Model and represents extensive fragmentation and the disintegration of the central core. The audience is

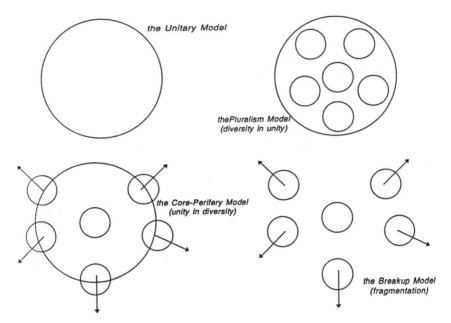

Figure 8.1. Four Stages of Audience Fragmentation
NOTE: Used with acknowledgment to Jan van Cuilenburg.

distributed over many different channels in no fixed pattern, and there is only sporadically shared audience experiences.

Despite the potential for progression through these stages, however, most audience attention in most countries remains fixed on a small number of general interest channels, and there is a good deal of overlap of audiences, with much sharing of popular content items. This is very much the current television situation in multi-cable channel countries. The core-periphery distribution stage has arrived (although not yet everywhere), but it does not lead to a significant growth of new and exclusive minority audiences. For most people, most of the time, the "core" still dominates their television use behavior. The reasons lie primarily in the near-universal appeal of mainstream content and the advantages to media organizations of continuing with mass provision, plus the continuing habits and patterns of social life. Media change is not enough on its own to disrupt established patterns of shared culture. While the final, breakup stage is certainly becoming more possible, it is still a hypothetical pattern and has not been realized.

Internationalization

The partial "escape" of the audience from the "surveillance" of the media organizations and institutions is also exemplified in the internationalization of media distribution, as noted already. Media transnationalization is not new and much has been written about it, especially in a critical spirit (see Sepstrup, 1989). The successive technologies of communication (the means of production) were diffused around the inhabited globe, following the lines of migration, religion, and colonization. One school of thought views the capture of audiences in Third World countries as a new form of cultural imperialism (see Tomlinson, 1991). A similar alarm has been expressed about the dominance of European audiovisual markets by American products and the loss of national and regional identity.

Whatever else, it is a fact that new audiences are being created in countries far from the place (and even time) of the original production and setting of the content. The new media are especially potent distributors of transnational media content, and much has been said about a global electronic superhighway, of which the Internet is a prototype. In principle, this network should be free of national control and accessible to all with the necessary equipment across the globe.

Despite the technological possibilities, the obstacles to extensive transnational audience formation remain very large. Domestic media retain an enormous advantage in availability and familiarity. They deal with the known world of the audience and they know their own audience. Language and culture account for most of the barriers and these are little affected by new technology (Biltereyst, 1992) or by reductions in cost. Western Europe provides an instructive case study, where nearly all the material and contextual factors favorable to internationalization are in place, yet where there is no pan-European audience at all to speak of, for any kind of medium of European origin, despite various initiatives in this direction. The nearest to an exception might be MTV Europe.

The much discussed "invasion" of Europe by American television has also been exaggerated and shows little in the way of an *increasing trend* (see McQuail, 1989, 1996; Varis, 1984). European television systems still need a constant supply of American film, fiction, and entertainment to fill their schedules and please their audiences, but these imports do not predominate in volume, even where markets are open, and do not overwhelm the perceived national character of the services in question (Hoskins & Mirus, 1988). Audiences do not find it hard to distinguish between imported and domestic products and "read" them differently (Biltereyst, 1991). The imports are incorporated into national media use patterns, often dubbed into the local language, and lose much of their alien character in the process.

Much more is known about the volume of American content transmitted on European television than about the size of actual audiences reached, although Sepstrup's (1989) research suggests that audience "exposure" to foreign programs is not as great as the amount offered suggests (see also Biltereyst, 1992). We have another case of supply outrunning consumption, which is typical of modern media conditions. New electronic technology has not yet made much headway against older barriers of poverty, ignorance, culture, ideology, and national control, all of which serve to restrain the globalizing process.

It is, nevertheless, possible that the homogeneity of audience experience over a large area of the globe is increasing, if only slowly. Media organizational practices and logic are often quite similar (the technology is, after all, the same) and there is much shared content. News coverage, for instance, follows much the same agenda in different countries. The latest Hollywood success or popular music hit is widely available and often imitated. International advertising contributes to the homogenizing process, although cultural differentiation by national market is still strong and unlikely to disappear. The homogenizing (or "synchronizing") trend (Hamelink, 1994) has been accelerated by the decline of communism and the opening to Western media of Eastern Europe and Russia. The developing world still continues to be a major recipient of Western media content, and new suppliers also arise.

Real changes are taking place in audience experience as a result of media globalization. It would be a mistake to think only in terms of the old "canonical audience" referred to above, since the nature of audience experience is also changing. It is quite plausible to suppose, although impossible to prove, that audience experience is less "national" than it used to be, as a result of several other changes including the "dilution" of culturally distinctive home-media products, as a result of imitating foreign models, styles, and media practices.

It is important to note the survival and even flowering of local and regional media, which have also benefited from the possibilities offered by new technologies of production and distribution (see Jankowski et al., 1992). We should also recall the cultural fragmentation and specialization that has led to numerous alternative identifications according to taste, interest, and subculture that are not particularly "national" in character (i.e., not "French," "Russian," "Irish," etc.). National definitions of cultural content are no longer exclusive or uniquely important. The context and setting of much media content remains culturally familiar, but there may be little distinctively related to the home country.

Conclusion

At the time of writing, the likely extent and speed of the "communications revolution" predicted on the basis of technological and other changes is very hard to gauge. Before striking a balance, we need to look a little more closely at the current challenges to the concept and reality of the media audience.

NINE

The Future of the Audience Concept

New Challenges

There is no doubt that the audience concept is in many ways outdated and its traditional role in communication theory, models, and research has been called into question. We can (and largely do) go on behaving as if the audience still exists "out there" somewhere, but we may be largely deceiving ourselves. The reasons for questioning the concept are both theoretical and pragmatic. In the early days of mass communication research, the audience concept stood for the body of actual or intended (often simultaneous) receivers of messages at the end of a linear process of information transmission. These usually constituted the paying media public for news and entertainment or the target for advertising and influence. This version has been gradually replaced by a view of the media receiver as more or less active, resistant to influence, and guided by his or her own concerns, depending on the particular social and cultural context. The communication process itself has been reconceptualized as essentially consultative, interactive, and transactional.

Equally important for theory is the relatively new idea that media audiences are typically "constructed" and selectively defined, according to a variety of different "logics" and discourses. The audience identified and sought by advertisers is not the same as that perceived by the actual media communicators (journalists, filmmakers, writers, etc.), nor the same as that which figures in discussions about politics, public opinion, media impact, and the "public interest." Media industry managers may, in turn, take a view of the audience that is different from these three. For them, the audience is a particular kind of consumer market with many subspecies. Another set of possibilities emerges when the audience is defined by people themselves according to their own interests, capacities, tastes, needs, preferences, and their social and cultural identities and experiences. When this perspective is taken, the diversity of possibilities for audience identification multiplies even more. We are dealing not with a single kind of social collectivity but with a great variety of different ones, all with a valid claim to be called an audience. This diverse set includes: media fans; social and political groups; ethnic groups; local communities; information consumers; special-interest groups; subcultures; lifestyles; taste cultures; market segments; and so on.

Among the pragmatic reasons for speaking of the "decline of the audience" is certainly the multiplication of media and channels. Attention to media sources is so diversified and dispersed in many directions that it makes no sense to speak or think any more in terms of a single or mass audience for "the media," or to refer to an entire population in their capacity as potential media users. It is not just that the mass audience has fragmented physically as a result of multiplication and abundance of media outlets (which is only true to a limited degree), but that the meanings of "audience" have multiplied. The largest potential change, even so, appears to stem from the emergence of really new kinds of media that do not have audiences at all in the old sense of spectators.

New Audiences for New Media?

Experience with the really new technologies is still at a very early stage. Early research has concentrated on the question of whether there is a sustainable demand of significant size for some of the new media, especially for interactive computer-based (videotex) services, virtual reality, and for all the new satellite television channels. The answers vary from place to place, depending mainly on local circumstances of availability and the wider media context

(Salvaggio & Bryant, 1989). The development of audiences for interactive media seems to depend also on the "critical mass" question—are there enough other subscribers to make it worthwhile being connected and to justify a diverse supply of information and other services? The problem here is that answers depend on there first being a critical mass (Markus, 1987; Oliver, Marwell, & Teixera, 1985).

A second aim of research has been to identify qualitative aspects of experience with the new media technology and to see how new media are rated. Among relevant factors are ease of use and "social presence" (Rice, 1984). Ease of use tends to increase as new media develop, following sufficient levels of adoption, but reliable evidence of how the quality of experience is perceived also depends on enough users having the experience. "Social presence" was first identified as a variable characteristic of audience (or user) experience with different kinds of media by Short, Williams, and Christie (1976).

Findings of research summarized by Rice (1984) show a predictable difference in degree of attributed "social presence" from the face-to-face conversation to the business letter. However, Rice (1984) observes that "social presence is at best a vague concept, never clearly defined by its proponents. Social presence is typically marked by such adjectives as 'social, sensitive, warm, and personal,' yet it is never explicitly operationalized" (p. 61).

Some comparative research on the images of old and new media by Perse and Courtright (1993) indicates that some of the "new media" such as VCRs, multichannel cable, or satellite are not really distinguished in audience perception from existing media, while computer-based media still stand alone and are not very positively valued, especially because they are impersonal and not (yet at least) associated with enjoyment. While the findings of early research on audience/user perceptions of different media are interesting, it is still hard to distinguish what is essentially due to a *medium* from what comes from the particular use or the context of use.

The extent of the potential appeal of *interactivity* in itself is still very uncertain. Interactivity has been defined by Neuman (1991) as "the quality of electronically mediated communications characterised by increased control over the communication process by both sender and receiver" (p. 104). It has usually been valued by media theorists, often implicitly in opposition to mass audience theory, because it denotes more self-control, choice, involvement, a richer experience, resistance to influence. In practice, interactivity is experienced in very diverse forms, not all of which live up to expectations.

For instance, it includes: video games; virtual reality; home shopping; Internet searches, postings, and matings; electronic voting; participation in game shows; home learning; off-track betting; being able to record and replay; looking up football results; and so on. It clearly extends the power of the audience member to intervene, to talk back and select, to gain access and it shakes up and diversifies audience experience, but it is not an alternative for the familiar "spectatorship" of the old mass media.

The Audience Lives On

Despite all this, as long as "mass media" remain, older meanings and older realities of audience will also remain current and relevant. The evidence for the decline of mass media is itself somewhat mixed, and the vast publicity machine of the media industry is no less geared to maximizing and maintaining the mass audience phenomenon, even as distribution channels have been multiplying. New media technology is not only being developed as an *alternative* to old media. Often the commercial and industrial parties to media innovation have their roots and their pocket books in the "old" media industries and are not seeking to compete with themselves, but to extend their power.

The provisional indications are that new developments, as they arrive (e.g., more channels, remote control, recording and replay) are assimilated easily into audience experience, perception, and behavior. The audience adapts to new opportunities and difficulties. For instance, extra channels create problems of choice, demanding new routines of choice making (see Ferguson & Perse, 1993; Heeter, 1988; Perse, 1990), but do not fundamentally change behavior. Viewers establish for themselves a limited repertoire of preferred channels, rather than distributing time over many channels.

In the United States, the spread of cable ate rapidly and heavily into the audience share of the three main TV networks, but this process halted and stabilized in 1993. Webster and Phalen (1997) note that, "It is apparent from currently available data that traditional mass appeal network television still dominates media consumption in the United States" (p. 114). In Europe, the impact of change has varied from country to country, but the dispersion of attention among channels has been marked by moderation and gradualness. Some of the "problems" created by technology, in the sense of disturbing old habits of media use, have been solved in part by the technology itself—for example, using recorders for time-shifting and acquiring additional receivers.

The most plausible conclusion that can be reached at the present state of innovation is that there is a very considerable inertial force that limits fundamental change in audience formation and behavior in the face of all those forces for change and technological potential. In his book, *The Future of the Mass Audience,* Neuman (1991) portrays the push of new information and communication technologies toward more diversity and participation as being resisted by two other powerful forces, one of which he names "the social psychology of media use," expressed in "deeply ingrained habits of passive, half-attentive media use" (p. 42). The other pressure is the (American) mass communications industry. Neuman argues that "Economies of scale push in the direction of common-denominator, one-way mass communications, rather than promoting narrowcasting and two-way communications" (p. 42).

This is an important part of the story, although the "psychology of the mass audience" and economic forces are not the only factors resisting or guiding the course of the communication revolution. To judge from the contents of the preceding chapter, there are also powerful and varied *social* forces in the context of media production and use that have much deeper roots and wider consequences. The shape of audiences still reflects the structure, dynamics, and needs of social formations ranging from societies to small groups. These forces do not all work in the same direction, and some are likely to be (maybe increasingly) favorable to new uses of new media and thus new audience realities. We cannot, therefore, make any certain predictions concerning the degree or limits of change.

We do not even know whether new and old forms of media will actually merge, according to the widely predicted technological possibilities of convergence. The same cable may soon bring many different (multimedia) opportunities to the same customers, but there is little reason to expect that the established distinctions of perception of media services according, for instance, to whether they are entertaining or useful, sociable or solitary, for personal/domestic use or for work and business, will quickly fade.

The extent to which newspapers and other print media offer their products and services on-line to Internet users, without any short-term profit, is an indication of the industry interest in retaining a grip on "their" audience. We should not expect the new media to subvert the old media order too fundamentally (Winston, 1986). In practice, the interactive potential of new technology is as likely to strengthen the position of the media "sender" as to serve the "empowerment" of receivers. The greater potential for interactivity of new electronic media is actually a force for consolidation of the traditional audience since it opens up new possibilities for active relations between senders and receivers (e.g., as with video-on-demand and the coming digital television).

The older idea that the media created their audiences is far from extinct, despite the greater scope for receiver influence and autonomy. This is not just the result of more skilful manipulation or of clever marketing and publicity. There are still performers, performances, news reports, documentaries that succeed day after day by way of press, film, video, radio, or television in uniting a body of spectators in something very much like the same cognitive or imaginative experience. Although it is correct to allow for large and numerous differences of interpretation, understanding, and application in daily life, the core experience is still recognizably a shared one and understood as such by most of those involved. Otherwise we could not explain the perennial success of "classics" and old favorites of all media and genres and the unexpected resonance and recognition that new "media products" can achieve. This is still the old process of "audience creation" at work, much as it was 200 years ago or more.

The theory of significant media events (Dayan & Katz, 1992) discussed earlier (see "The Public and Private Spheres of Media Use" in Chapter 6) is a reminder that society itself has not changed so fundamentally in the era of mass media and the early phases of the information society. There are still nation-states, strong collective identities, and wide communities of interest that continue to provide the potential for the formation of large and also engaged audiences. The media have become an important means of expression for collective identities and allegiances, nationally and globally, and a major means for their enforcement.

Democratic political processes also help to sustain the traditional relation between media and audiences defined as publics, despite much criticism of manipulative political marketing. Parties and advocacy groups need to target and reach potential supporters by way of more or less independent media that act as gatekeepers for specific kinds of audience.

There is plenty of evidence that campaigners see the new media simply as an extra opportunity for doing this work. Voters still need information on which to base opinions on ever-changing issues. They still seek this information in their capacity as media audiences, and they, too, use the new media for "traditional" purposes.

Last, but not least, the mass media have arisen partly as a vehicle for mass commercial advertising, and the role of advertising has, if anything, grown. While mature markets require more diversified and better targeted advertising, there is still a large sector of advertising (especially in emerging markets) that needs the possibility of reaching large mass publics with simple messages concerning simple consumer products. It is most unlikely that this need will be allowed to go unmet.

Some Conceptual Issues

Although we can be fairly sure of much continuity in mass communication audience realities, current changes do represent a significant challenge to lazy thinking about this key concept in the study of communication. Some of these challenges have been thoughtfully examined by Morris and Ogan (1996), with particular reference to the following matters: the interactive features of new media; the problem of what now constitutes a *mass* in audience terms; the issue of credibility of media sources; the relationship between personal and mass communication; and the degree to which *interchangeability* of producer and receiver roles can and does take place. Their main conclusion concerning the Internet is that its communication forms offer a long continuum of possibilities, ranging from dyadic interaction to the traditional model of mass communication. This means that the roles of audience members are also varied and numerous and we learn to move from one to another.

It still seems helpful to consider the changing and expanding forms of communication by using the general term *audience* to refer to those who are *reached* by (or brought into contact with) a given *communication medium,* whatever the precise character of their involvement. For present purposes a "communication medium" can be defined as any organizational form or device that is designed to facilitate the giving, taking, sharing, exchanging, or storing of meaning. It is not necessary to decide precisely what to include within this definition, since this can be left to usage and convention and the range of candidate media is continually widening.

At first sight it does not seem to make much sense to speak of the many sets of users of interactive media as audiences, especially when the usual boundaries provided by physical time, place, and attention to fixed objects are no longer in place or visible. In many languages, the term *audience* cannot be divested of its strong connotation of people sitting, watching, and listening. The classic meaning of the audience term has always been *message related,* while theory and experience have come to recognize the near-equal significance of *behavioral* and also the *social, emotional, and affective* aspects of media use—the intrinsic pleasures and satisfactions of the process of using media in various contexts.

Probably new terms (or new usages of old ones) will need to be developed for some genuinely new kinds of communication participant groups, perhaps differentiated according to types of new media use. But we still cannot rule out the term *audience* for the consumers of standardized software supplied through multimedia channels. The extent of adaptation in usage and new conceptual development may depend on how far we remain sensitive to the original connotation of the audience term as a body of listeners or spectators and how far this meaning actually persists in reality. The notion of an "active audience" has, it seems, already been incorporated without too much difficulty into the terminology concerning media "consumption" and use behavior.

Audience Types and Terms: A Closing Word

The possibilities for formation of new types of audience are now so numerous that no single typology can do justice to the reality. It is hard to imagine any word that can cover the situations of media exposure, ranging from in-flight movies to messages inscribed on every conceivable item that catches our attention. Even so, theory and research on the audience allows us to designate a limited number of key dimensions according to which the variety of audiences can be mapped out. These dimensions of audience type are also potential variables in empirical research into audience behavior. While new variables are added as media develop and the relative significance of older variables changes, there is a good deal of continuity in the conceptual apparatus of audience theory and research.

As a reminder of some of the main themes of this book, we can summarily present the most important variable characteristics of audiences that have emerged. The items shown in Table 9.1 are mixed in origin, referring variously to: measurable physical features; activity and process; context and situation; mental perceptions and impressions on the part of those involved. Further

TABLE 9.1 The Main Dimensions of Audience

- Degree of activity or passivity
- Degree of interactivity and interchangeability
- Size and duration
- Locatedness in space
- Group character (social/cultural identity)
- Simultaneity of contact with source
- Heterogeneity of composition
- Social relations between sender and receiver
- Message vs. social/behavioral definition of situation
- Degree of "social presence"
- Sociability of context of use

dimensions would need to be added if detailed account were to be taken of inter-media differences.

Each of the variables indicated can be used to describe and classify the myriad kinds of audiences that are now to be encountered, although not all are relevant for every purpose. Each entry in Table 9.1 has a lineage that extends back to the original historical audience of spectators and listeners that preceded the mass media. On this basis we can argue both for continuity in the nature of audience experience and for the relevance of past thinking to ongoing tasks of analysis and interpretation. No doubt new and more specific terms will emerge for particular purposes.

The drift of these remarks is in favor of keeping the old term *audience* and making use of an already rich terminology for referring to the different kinds of socially, culturally, behaviorally, linguistically, and economically defined audience phenomena that are now proliferating. We can no longer use the term without giving a clear indication of what we mean by it in a given instance, and any "measure" of audience will have to be understood in a specific way. But that advice should always have been followed and it is the main justification for this book.

References

Alasuutari, P. (1992). "I'm ashamed to admit it but I have watched Dallas." The moral hierarchy of television programmes. *Media Culture and Society, 14*(1), 561-582.

Alberoni, F. (1972). The "powerless elite": Theory and sociological research on the phenomenon of the stars. In D. McQuail (Ed.), *Sociology of mass communication* (pp. 75-98). Harmondsworth, UK: Penguin.

Allen, R. C. (1989). "Soap opera," audiences and the limits of genre. In E. Seiter, H. Borchers, G. Kreutzner, & E.-M. Warth (Eds.), *Remote control* (pp. 4-55). London: Routledge & Kegan Paul.

Anderson, J., Collins, P. A., Schmitt, R. S., & Jacobovitz, R. S. (1996). Stressful life events and television viewing. *Communication Research, 23*(3), 243-260.

Ang, I. (1985). *Watching Dallas: Soap opera and the melodramatic imagination.* London: Methuen.

Ang, I. (1991). *Desperately seeking the audience.* London. Routledge & Kegan Paul.

Austen, P. J. (1992). Television that talks back: An experimental validation of a PSI scale. *Journal of Broadcasting and Electronic Media, 36*(1), 173-181.

Avery, R. (1979). Adolescents' use of the mass media. *American Behavioral Scientist, 23,* 53-70.

Avery, R. (1993). *Public service broadcasting.* New York: Longman.

Babrow, A. S. (1988). Theory and method in research on audience motives. *Journal of Broadcasting and Electronic Media, 32*(4), 471-487.

Ball-Rokeach, S., & DeFleur, M. (1976). A dependency model of mass media effects. *Communication Research, 3,* 3-21.

Bandini, T. (1995). The social construction of the personal computer user. *Journal of Communication, 45*(3), 40-65.

Barnes, B. E., & Thomson, L. M. (1994). Power to the people (meter): Audience measurement technology and media specialization. In J. S. Ettema & D. C. Whitney (Eds.), *Audiencemaking: How the media create the audience* (pp. 75-94). Thousand Oaks, CA: Sage.

Barwise, P., & Ehrenberg, A. (1988). *Television and its audience.* London: Sage.

Bauer, R. A. (1964a). The communicator and the audience. In L. A. Dexter & D. M. White (Eds.), *People, society, and mass communication* (pp. 125-139). New York: Free Press.

Bauer, R. A. (1964b). The obstinate audience. *American Psychologist, 19,* 319-328.

Bausinger, H. (1984). Media, technology and daily life. *Media, Culture and Society, 6*(4), 343-351.

Becker, L. B., Kosicki, G. M., & Jones, F. (1992). Racial differences in evaluations of the mass media. *Journalism Quarterly, 69*(1), 124-134.

Belsey, A., & Chadwick, R. (Eds.). (1992). *Ethical issues in journalism.* London: Routledge & Kegan Paul.

Beniger, J. R. (1986). *The control revolution.* Cambridge, MA: Harvard University Press.

Berelson, B. (1949). What missing the newspaper means. In P. F. Lazarsfeld & F. Stanton (Eds.), *Communication research 1948-9* (pp. 111-129). New York: Duell, Sloan and Pearce.

Biltereyst, D. (1991). Regulating American hegemony: A comparative analysis of the reception of domestic and U.S. fiction. *European Journal of Communication, 6*(4), 469-497.

Biltereyst, D. (1992). Language and culture as ultimate barriers? An examination of the circulation and consumption of fiction in small European countries. *European Journal of Communication, 7*(4), 517-540.

Biocca, F. A. (1988a). The breakdown of the canonical audience. In J. Anderson (Ed.), *Communication yearbook 11* (pp. 127-132). Newbury Park, CA: Sage.

Biocca, F. A. (1988b). Opposing conceptions of the audience. In J. Anderson (Ed.), *Communication yearbook 11* (pp. 51-80). Newbury Park, CA: Sage.

Blanchard, M. A. (1977). The Hutchins Commission, the press, and the responsibility concept. *Journalism Monographs, 49.*

Blumer, H. (1933). *Movies and conduct.* New York: Macmillan.

Blumer, H. (1946). The mass, the public, and public opinion. In A. Lee (Ed.), *New outlines of the principles of sociology* (pp. 167-222). New York: Barnes & Noble.

Blumler, J. G., & Katz, E. (Eds.). (1974). *The uses of mass communications.* Beverly Hills, CA: Sage.

Blumler, J. G. (1985). The social character of media gratifications. In K. E. Rosengren, P. Palmgreen, & L. Wenner (Eds.), *Media gratification research: Current perspectives* (pp. 41-59). Beverly Hills, CA: Sage.

Blumler, J. G., & McQuail, D. (1968). *Television in politics: Its uses and influence.* London: Faber.

Blumler, J. G., & Mitchell, J. (Eds.). (1994). *Television and the viewer interest.* London: John Libbey.

Bogart, L. (1995). *Commercial culture.* New York: Oxford University Press.

Bordewijk, J. L., & van Kaam, B. (1986). Towards a new classification of tele-information services. *Intermedia, 14*(1), 16-21. (Reprinted from *Allocutie,* 1982, Baarn: Bosch and Keuning)

Bourdieu, P. (1984). *Distinction: A social critique of the judgement of taste.* London: Routledge & Kegan Paul.

Brown, J. W. (Ed.). (1976). *Children and television.* London: Collier-Macmillan.

Brown, J. R., & Linne, O. (1976). The family as a mediator of television's effects. In J. R. Brown (Ed.), *Children and television.* London: Collier-Macmillan.

Burnett, R. (1990). *Concentration and diversity in the international phonogram industry.* Gothenburg, Sweden: University of Gothenburg.

Burns, T. (1969). Public service and private world. In P. Halmos (Ed.), *The sociology of mass media communicators* (pp. 53-73). Keele, Staffordshire, UK: University of Keele.

Canary, D. J., & Spitzberg, R. H. (1993). Loneliness and media gratifications. *Communication Research, 20*(6), 800-821.

Cantor, M. (1971). *The Hollywood television producers.* New York: Basic Books.

Cantor, M. (1994). The role of the audience in the production of culture. In J. S. Ettema & D. C. Whitney (Eds.), *Audiencemaking: How the media create the audience* (pp. 159-170). Thousand Oaks CA: Sage.

Cantril, H., & Allport, G. (1935). *The psychology of radio.* New York: Harper.

Carey, J. (1975). A cultural approach to communication. *Communication, 2,* 1-22.

Carey, J. (1977). Mass communication research and cultural studies: An American view. In J. Curran, M. Gurevitch, & J. Woollacott (Eds.), *Mass communication and society* (pp. 409-426). London: Edward Arnold.

Carey, J. W., with Kreiling, A. L. (1974). Popular culture and uses and gratifications. In J. G. Blumler & E. Katz (Eds.), *The uses of mass communications* (pp. 225-248). Beverly Hills, CA: Sage.

Christensen, P., & Peterson, J. B. (1988). Genre and gender in the structure of music preferences. *Communication Research, 15*(3), 282-301.

Christians, C. G., & Rotzell, K. B. (1991). *Media ethics: Cases and moral reasoning.* New York: Longman.

Clausse, R. (1968). The mass public at grips with mass communication. *International Social Science Journal, 20*(4), 625-643.

Comstock, G. (1988). Today's audience, tomorrow's media. In S. Oskamp (Ed.), *Television as a social issue* (pp. 324-345). Newbury Park, CA: Sage.

Comstock, G., Chaffee, S., Katzman, N., McCombs, M., & Roberts, D. (Eds.). (1978). *Television and human behavior.* New York: Columbia University Press.

Conway, J. C., & Rubin, A. M. (1991). Psychological predictors of television viewing motivation. *Communication Research, 18*(4), 443-463.

Cooley, C. H. (1908). *Human nature and the social order.* New York: Scribner.

Cooper, R. (1993). An expanded, integrated model for determining audience exposure to television. *Journal of Broadcasting and Electronic Media, 37*(4), 401-418.

Cooper, R. (1996). The status and future of audience duplication research. *Journal of Broadcasting and Electronic Media, 40*(1), 96-111.

Curran, J. (1990). The new revisionism in mass communication research: A reappraisal. *European Journal of Communication, 5*(2/3), 135-164.

Dayan, D., & Katz, E. (1992). *Media events.* Cambridge, MA: Harvard University Press.

DeFleur, M. L. (1970). *Theories of mass communication* (2nd ed.). New York: David McKay.

Delia, J. G. (1987). Communication research: A history. In S. H. Chaffee & C. Berger (Eds.), *Handbook of communication* (pp. 20-98). Newbury Park, CA: Sage.

Dimmick, J. W., Sikard, J., & Patterson, S. J. (1994). The gratifications of the telephone: Sociability, instrumentality and reassurance. *Communication Research, 21*(5), 643-663.

Donohew, L., Palmgreen, P., & Rayburn, J. D. (1987). Social and psychological origins of media use: A lifestyle analysis. *Journal of Broadcasting and Electronic Media, 31*(3), 255-278.

Downing, J. (1984). *Radical media.* Boston: South End.

Drew, D., & Weaver, D. (1990). Media attention, media exposure, and media effects. *Journalism Quarterly, 67*(4), 740-748.

Dutton, W., Blumler, J. G., & Kramer, S. (Eds.). (1987). *Wired cities. Shaping the future of communication.* Washington, DC: Knowledge Industries.

Eastman, S. T. (1979). Uses of television viewing and consumer life styles: A multivariate analysis. *Journal of Broadcasting, 23,* 491-500.

Elliott, P. (1972). *The making of a television series: A case study in the production of culture.* London: Constable.

Elliott, P. (1974). Uses and gratifications research: A critique and a sociological alternative. In J. G. Blumler & E. Katz (Eds.), *The uses of mass communications* (pp. 249-268). Beverly Hills, CA: Sage.

Emmett, B. P. (1968). A new role for research in broadcasting. *Public Opinion Quarterly, 32,* 554-665.

Emmett, B. P. (1972). The TV and radio audience in Britain. In D. McQuail (Ed.), *Sociology of mass communications* (pp. 195-217). Harmondsworth, UK: Penguin.

Engel, J., & Blackwell, R. (1982). *Consumer behavior.* Chicago: Holt Saunders.

Ennis, P. H. (1961). The social structure of communication systems. *Studies in Public Communication, 3,* 120-144.

Enzensberger, H. M. (1972). Constituents of a theory of the media. In D. McQuail (Ed.), *Sociology of mass communication* (pp. 99-116). Harmondsworth, UK: Penguin. (Reprinted from *New Left Review, 64,* 1970, pp. 13-36)

Espé, H., & Seiwert, M. (1986). European television viewer types: A six nation classification by programme interest. *European Journal of Communication, 1*(3), 301-325.

Ettema, J. S., & Whitney, D. C. (Eds.). (1982). *Individuals in mass media organizations.* Beverly Hills, CA: Sage.

Fallows, J. (1996). *Breaking the news: How the mass media undermine American democracy.* New York: Pantheon.

Febvre, L., & Martin, H. D. (1984). *The coming of the book.* London: Verso.

Feilitzen, C. von (1976). The functions served by the mass media. In J. W. Brown (Ed.), *Children and television.* London: Collier-Macmillan.

Ferguson, D. A., & Perse, E. M. (1993). Media audience influences on channel repertoire. *Journal of Broadcasting and Electronic Media, 37*(1), 31-47.

Ferguson, M. (1983). *Forever feminine: Women's magazines and the cult of femininity.* London: Heinemann.

Ferguson, M. (1992). The mythology about globalization. *European Journal of Communication, 7*(2), 69-83.

Ferguson, M., & Golding, P. (Eds.). (1997). *Cultural studies in question.* London: Sage.

Finn, C. (1992). TV addiction? An evaluation of four competing media use models. *Journalism Quarterly, 69,* 422-435.

Finn, S., & Gomm, M. B. (1988). Social isolation and social support as correlates of television viewing motivations. *Communication Research, 15*(2), 135-158.

Fiske, J. (1987). *Television culture.* London: Methuen.

Fiske, J. (1992). The cultural economy of fandom. In L. Lewis (Ed.), *The adoring audience: Fan culture and popular media* (pp. 30-59). London: Routledge & Kegan Paul.

Frachon, C., & Vargaftig, M. (Eds.). (1995). *European television: Immigrants and ethnic minorities.* London: John Libbey.

Frank, R. E., & Greenberg, B. (1980). *The public's view of television.* Beverly Hills, CA: Sage.

Freidson, E. (1953). Communication research and the concept of the mass. *American Sociological Review, 18*(3), 313-317.

Frissen, V. (1992). Trapped in electronic cages? Gender and new information technology. *Media, Culture and Society, 14,* 31-50.

Frith, S., & Goodwin, A. (Eds.). (1990). *On record.* London: Routledge & Kegan Paul.

Gandy, O. (1989). The surveillance society: Information technologies and bureaucratic social control. *Journal of Communication, 39*(3), 61-76.

Gans, H. (1957). The creator-audience relationship in the mass media. In B. Rosenberg & D. M. White (Eds.), *Mass culture* (pp. 315-324). New York: Free Press.

Gans, H. J. (1979). *Deciding what's news.* New York: Vintage.

Gaziano, C., & McGrath, K. (1987). Newspaper credibility and relationships of newspaper journalists to communities. *Journalism Quarterly, 64,* 317-328.

Geiger, K., & Sokol, R. (1959). Social norms in watching television. *American Journal of Sociology, 65*(3), 178-181.

Geraghty, C. (1991). *Women and soap opera.* Cambridge, UK: Polity Press.

Gerbner, G., Gross, L., Morgan, M., Signorielli, N., & Jackson-Beek, M. (1979). The demonstration of power: Violence Profile No. 10. *Journal of Communication, 29*(3), 177-196.

Gillespie, M. (1995). *Television, ethnicity and cultural change.* London: Routledge & Kegan Paul.

Gitlin, T. (1978). Media sociology: The dominant paradigm. *Theory and Society, 6,* 205-253.

Golding, P., & van Snippenburg, L. (1995). Government, communications and the media. In *Beliefs in government* (Vol. 3). London: Oxford University Press.

Graber, D. (1984). *Processing the news.* New York: Longman.

Gray, H. (1992). Television, black Americans, and the American dream. In H. Newcomb (Ed.), *Television: The critical view* (5th ed., pp. 170-187). New York: Oxford University Press.

Greenberg, B. S. (1964). Person-to-person communication in the diffusion of a news event. *Journalism Quarterly, 41,* 489-494.

Gunter, B. (1987). *Poor reception.* Hillsdale, NJ: Lawrence Erlbaum.

Gunter, B., & Winstone, P. (1993). *Television: The public's view.* London: John Libbey.

Hall, S. (1977). Culture, the media and the "ideological effect." In J. Curran, M. Gurevitch, & J. Woollacott (Eds.), *Mass communication and society* (pp. 315-348). London: Edward Arnold.

Hall, S. (1980). Coding and encoding in the television discourse. In S. Hall et al. (Eds.), *Culture, media, language.* London: Hutchinson.

Hall, S., & Jefferson, T. (1975). *Resistance through rituals.* London: Hutchinson.

Halloran, J. D., Brown, R. L., & Chaney, D. C. (1970). *Television and delinquency.* Leicester, UK: Leicester University Press.

Hamelink, C. (1994). *The politics of world communication.* London: Sage.

Handel, L. (1950). *Hollywood looks at its audience.* Urbana: University of Illinois Press.

Hart, H. (1991). *Critical communication studies.* New York: Routledge.

Hawkins, R. P., Reynolds, N., & Pingree, S. (1991). In search of television viewing styles. *Journal of Broadcasting and Electronic Media, 35*(3), 375-383.

Hebdige, D. (1978). *Subculture: The meaning of style.* London: Methuen.

Hedinsson, E. (1981). *TV, family and society: The social origins and effects of adolescents' TV use.* Stockholm: Almqvist & Wiksell International.

Heeter, C. (1988). The choice process model. In C. Heeter & B. Greenberg (Eds.), *Cableviewing* (pp. 11-32). Norwood, NJ: Ablex.

Hermes, J. (1995). *Reading women's magazines.* Cambridge, UK: Polity Press.

Herzog, H. (1953). What do we really know about day-time serial listeners? In B. Berelson & M. Janowitz (Eds.), *Reader in public opinion and communication* (pp. 352-365). New York: Free Press. (Reprinted from P. F. Lazarsfeld & F. Stanton, Eds., [1944] *Radio research 1942-3,* New York: Duell, Sloan and Pearce)

Himmelweit, H. T., & Swift, T. (1976). Continuities and discontinuities in media taste. *Journal of Social Issues, 32*(6), 332-356.

Himmelweit, H. T., Vince, P., & Oppenheim, A. N. (1958). *Television and the child.* London: Oxford University Press.

Hobson, D. (1982). *Crossroads: The drama of a soap opera.* London: Methuen.

Hobson, D. (1989). Soap operas at work. In E. Seiter, H. Borchers, G. Kreutzner, & E.-M. Warth (Eds.), *Remote control* (pp. 150-167). London: Routledge & Kegan Paul.

Hoggart, R. (1957). *The uses of literacy.* London: Chatto & Windus.

Hopkins, M. (1970). *Mass media in the Soviet Union.* New York: Pegasus.

Horton, D., & Wohl, R. R. (1956). Mass communication and para-social interaction. *Psychiatry, 19,* 215-229.

Hoskins, C., & Mirus, R. (1988). Reasons for the U.S. dominance of the international trade in television programmes. *Media, Culture and Society, 10,* 499-515.

Hoskins, C., Mirus, R., & Rozeboom, W. (1989). U.S. television programs in the international market: Unfair pricing? *Journal of Communication, 39*(2), 55-75.

Hovland, C. I., Lumsdaine, A. A., & Sheffeld, F. D. (1949). *Experiments in mass communication.* Princeton, NJ: Princeton University Press.

Hyman, H. H., & Sheatsley, P. (1947). Some reasons why information campaigns fail. *Public Opinion Quarterly, 11,* 412-423.

Jankowski, N., Prehn, O., & Stappers, J. (Eds.). (1992). *The people's voice.* London: John Libbey.

Janowitz, M. (1952). *The community press in an urban setting.* Glencoe, IL: Free Press.

Jay, M. (1973). *The dialectical imagination.* London: Heinemann.

Jensen, K. B. (1988). News as a social resource. *European Journal of Communication, 3*(3), 275-301.

Jensen, K. B. (1991). When is meaning? Communication theory, pragmatism, and mass media reception. In J. Anderson (Ed.), *Communication yearbook 14* (pp. 3-32). Newbury Park, CA: Sage.

Jensen, K. B., & Rosengren, K. E. (1990). Five traditions in search of the audience. *European Journal of Communication, 5*(2-3), 207-238.

Jhally, S., & Livant, B. (1986). Watching as working: The valorization of audience consciousness. *Journal of Communication, 36*(2), 124-163.

Johansson, T., & Miegel, F. (1992). *Do the right thing*. Stockholm: Almqvist & Wiksell International.

Jones, P. (Ed.). (1995). *CyberSociety: Computer mediated communication and community*. Thousand Oaks, CA: Sage.

Jowett, G., & Linton, J. M. (1980). *Movies as mass communication*. Beverly Hills, CA: Sage.

Katz, E., Blumler, J. G., & Gurevitch, M. (1974). Utilization of mass communication by the individual. In J. G. Blumler & E. Katz (Eds.), *The uses of mass communication* (pp. 19-32). Beverly Hills, CA: Sage.

Katz, E., & Foulkes, D. (1962). On the use of mass media as "escape": Clarification of a concept. *Public Opinion Quarterly, 26*(3), 361-376.

Katz, E., Gurevitch, M., & Haas, H. (1973). On the use of mass media for important things. *American Sociological Review, 38*, 164-181.

Katz, E., & Lazarsfeld, P. F. (1955). *Personal influence*. Glencoe, IL: Free Press.

Kaufer, D. S., & Carley, K. M. (1993). *Communication at a distance*. Hillsdale, NJ: Lawrence Erlbaum.

Kippax, S., & Murray, J. P. (1980). Using the mass media: Need gratification and perceived utility. *Communication Research, 7*(3), 335-360.

Klapper, J. (1960). *The effects of mass communication*. New York: Free Press.

Kleinsteuber, H., & Sonnenberg, U. (1990). Beyond public service and private profit: International experience with non-commercial local radio. *European Journal of Communication, 5*(1), 87-106.

Krcmar, M. (1996). Family communication patterns, discourse behavior and child TV viewing. *Human Communication Research, 23*(2), 251-277.

Krugman, H. (1965). The impact of television advertising: Learning without involvement. *Public Opinion Quarterly, 29*, 349-356.

Kubey, R. W. (1986). Television use in everyday life: Coping with unstructured time. *Journal of Communication, 36*, 108-123.

Kubey, R., & Csikszentmihalyi, M. (1991). *Television and the quality of life*. Hillsdale, NJ: Lawrence Erlbaum.

Lazarsfeld, P. F., Berelson, B., & Gaudet, H. (1944). *The people's choice*. New York: Columbia University Press.

Lazarsfeld, P. F., & Field, H. (Eds.). (1946). *The people look at radio*. Chapel Hill: University of North Carolina Press.

Lazarsfeld, P. F., & Stanton, F. (Eds.). (1944). *Radio research 1942-3*. New York: Duell, Sloan and Pearce.

Lazarsfeld, P. F., & Stanton, F. (Eds.). (1949). *Communication research 1948/9*. New York: Harper & Bros.

Leggatt, T. (1991). Identifying the undefinable. *Studies of Broadcasting, 27*, 113-132.

Levy, M. R. (1978). The audience experience with television news. *Journalism Monographs, 55*.

Levy, M. R., & Windahl, S. (1985). The concept of audience activity. In K. E. Rosengren, P. Palmgreen, & L. Wenner (Eds.), *Media gratification research: Current perspectives* (pp. 109-122). Beverly Hills, CA: Sage.

Lewis, G. H. (1981). Taste cultures and their composition: Towards a new theoretical perspective. In E. Katz & T. Szecsko (Eds.), *Mass media and social change* (pp. 201-217). London: Sage.

Lewis, G. H. (1992). Who do you love? The dimensions of musical taste. In J. Lull (Ed.), *Popular music and communication* (2nd ed., pp. 134-151). Newbury Park, CA: Sage.

Lewis, L. (1992). *The adoring audience: Fan culture and popular media*. London: Routledge & Kegan Paul.

Lichtenstein, S. L., & Rosenfeld, L. B. (1983). Uses and misuses of gratifications research: An explication of media functions. *Communications Research, 10*, 97-109.

Liebes, T., & Katz, E. (1986). Patterns of involvement in television fiction: A comparative analysis. *European Journal of Communication, 1*(2), 151-172.

Liebes, T., & Katz, E. (1989). Critical abilities of TV viewers. In E. Seiter, H. Borchers, G. Kreutzner, & E.-M. Warth (Eds.), *Remote control* (pp. 204-222). London: Routledge & Kegan Paul.

Liebes, T., & Katz, E. (1990). *The export of meaning: Cross-cultural readings of Dallas*. Oxford, UK: Oxford University Press.

Lindlof, T. (1988). Media audiences as interpretive communities. In J. Anderson (Ed.), *Communication yearbook 11* (pp. 81-107). Newbury Park, CA: Sage.

Lindlof, T. (1991). The qualitative study of media audiences. *The Journal of Broadcasting and Electronic Media, 35*(1), 23-42.

Livingstone, S. M. (1988). Why people watch soap opera: An analysis of the explanations of British viewers. *European Journal of Communication, 3*(1), 55-80.

Livingstone, S. M., & Lunt, P. (1994). *Talk on television: Audience participation and public debate*. London: Routledge & Kegan Paul.

Lombard, M. (1995). Direct response to people on the screen. *Communication Research, 22*(3), 288-324.

Lull, J. (1982a). How families select television programs. *The Journal of Broadcasting and Electronic Media, 26*(4), 801-811.

Lull, J. (1982b). The social uses of television. *Human Communication Research, 6*(3), 197-208. Beverly Hills (CA) and London: Sage. (Also in D. C. Whitney et al., Eds., *Mass communication review yearbook, 1982*, pp. 397-409, Beverly Hills (CA) and London: Sage)

Lull, J. (Ed.). (1992). *Popular music and communication*. Newbury Park, CA: Sage.

Maccoby, E. (1954). Why do children watch TV? *Public Opinion Quarterly, 18,* 239-244.

Maisel, R. (1973). The decline of mass media. *Public Opinion Quarterly, 37,* 159-170.

Marcuse, H. (1964). *One dimensional man*. London: Routledge & Kegan Paul.

Markus, M. L. (1987). Towards a "critical mass" theory of interactive media. *Communication Research, 14*(5), 491-511.

Martel, M. U., & McCall, G. J. (1964). Reality-orientation and the pleasure principle. In L. A. Dexter & D. M. White (Eds.), *People, society and mass communication* (pp. 283-333). New York: Free Press.

Marvin, C. (1988). *When old technologies were new*. New York: Oxford University Press.

Maslow, A. (1968). *Towards a sociology of being*. New York: Van Nostrand.

McCain, T. (1986). Patterns of media use in Europe. *European Journal of Communication, 1*(3), 231-250.

McDonald, D. G. (1990). Media orientation and television news viewing. *Journalism Quarterly, 67*(1), 11-20.

McDonald, D. G., & Schechter, R. (1988). Audience role in the evolution of fictional TV content. *Journal of Broadcasting, 32*(1), 419-440.

McGuigan, P. (1992). *Cultural populism*. London: Routledge & Kegan Paul.

McGuire, W. J. (1974). Psychological motives and communication gratifications. In J. G. Blumler & E. Katz (Eds.), *The uses of mass communications* (pp. 167-196). Beverly Hills, CA: Sage.

McLeod, J., Daily, K., Guo, Z., Eveland, W. P., Bayer, J., Yang, S., & Wang, H. (1996). Community integration, local media use and democratic processes. *Communication Research, 23*(2), 179-210.

McLeod, J., & McDonald, D. G. (1985). Beyond simple exposure: Media orientations and their impact on political processes. *Communication Research, 12,* 3-32.

McLeod, M. J., Ward, L. S., & Tancill, K. (1965). Alienation and uses of mass media. *Public Opinion Quarterly, 29,* 583-594.

McQuail, D. (1984). With the benefit of hindsight: Reflections on uses and gratifications research. *Critical Studies in Mass Communication, 1*(2), 177-193.

McQuail, D. (1989). Commercial imperialism and cultural cost. In C. W. Thomson (Ed.), *Cultural transfer or electronic colonialism?* (pp. 207-217). Heidelberg: Carl Winter Universitätsverlag.

McQuail, D. (1994). *Mass communication theory: An introduction*. London: Sage.

McQuail, D. (1996). Transatlantic TV flows: A new look at cultural cost-accounting. In A. van Hemel (Ed.), *Trading culture* (pp. 111-125). Amsterdam: Boekman Foundation.

McQuail, D., Blumler, J. G., & Brown, J. W. (1972). The television audience, a revised perspective. In D. McQuail (Ed.), *Sociology of mass communications* (pp. 135-164). Harmondsworth, UK: Penguin.

McQuail, D., & Gurevitch, M. (1974). Explaining audience behavior. In J. G. Blumler & E. Katz (Eds.), *The uses of mass communication* (pp. 287-386). Beverly Hills, CA: Sage.

McQuail, D., & Windahl, S. (1993). *Communication models* (2nd ed.). London: Longman.

Mead, G. H. (1934). *Mind, self, and society*. Chicago: University of Chicago Press.

Mendelsohn, H. (1964). Listening to radio. In L. A. Dexter & D. M. White (Eds.), *People, society, and mass communication* (pp. 239-248). New York: Free Press.

Merton, R. K. (1949). Patterns of influence. In *Social theory and social structure* (pp. 387-470). Glencoe, IL: Free Press.

Meyrowitz, J. (1986). Television and interpersonal behavior: Codes of perception and response. In G. Gumpert & R. Cathcart (Eds.), *Inter/media: Interpersonal communication in a media world* (3rd ed., pp. 253-272). New York: Oxford University Press.

Mills, C. W. (1951). *White collar*. New York: Oxford University Press.

Mills, C. W. (1956). *The power elite*. New York: Oxford University Press.

Mitchell, A. (1983). *The nine American lifestyles*. New York: Warner Books.

Montgomery, K. C. (1989). *Target: Prime-time*. New York: Oxford University Press.

Moores, S. (1993). *Interpreting audiences*. London: Sage.

Morley, D. (1980). *The nationwide audience: Structure and decoding*. London: British Film Institute.

Morley, D. (1986). *Family television*. London: Routledge & Kegan Paul.

Morley, D. (1992). *Television, audiences and cultural studies*. London: Routledge & Kegan Paul.

Morris, M., & Ogan, C. (1996). The Internet as mass medium. *Journal of Communication, 46*(1), 39-50.

Murdock, G., & Phelps, G. (1973). *Mass media and the secondary school*. London: Macmillan.

Mytton, G., & Forrester, C. (1988). Audiences for international radio broadcasting. *European Journal of Communication, 3*(3), 457-481.

National Advertising Bureau (NAB). (1982). *The newspaper in people's minds* (Research Report). New York: Author.

National Advertising Bureau (NAB). (1984). *Meeting readers' multiple needs* (Research Report). New York: Author.

Negus, K. (1992). *Producing pop*. London: Edward Arnold.

Neuman, W. R. (1991). *The future of the mass audience*. Cambridge, UK: Cambridge University Press.

Neuman, W. R., & Pool, I. de Sola. (1986). The flow of communication into the home. In S. Ball-Rokeach & M. Cantor (Eds.), *Media, audience, and social structure* (pp. 71-86). Newbury Park, CA: Sage.

Newcomb, H. (1976). *Television: The critical view*. New York: Oxford University Press.

Noble, G. (1975). *Children in front of the small screen*. London: Constable.

Nord, D. P. (1995). Reading the newspaper: Strategies and politics of reader response, Chicago 1912-1917. *Journal of Communication, 45*(3), 66-93.

Oliver, P., Marwell, G., & Teixera, R. (1985). A theory of the critical mass. *American Journal of Sociology, 91*(3), 522-556.

Padioleau, J. (1985). *Le Monde et le Washington Post*. Paris: PUF.

Palmgreen, P., & Rayburn, J. D. (1985). An expectancy-value approach to media gratification. In K. E. Rosengren, P. Palmgreen, & L. Wenner (Eds.), *Media gratification research: Current perspectives* (pp. 61-73). Beverly Hills, CA: Sage.

Palmgreen, P., Wenner, L., & Rayburn, J. (1980). Relations between gratifications sought and obtained. A study of television news. *Communication Research, 7*(2), 161-192.

Pearlin, L. (1959). Social and personal stress and escape television viewing. *Public Opinion Quarterly, 23*, 255-259.

Perse, E. M. (1990). Audience selectivity and involvement in the newer media environment. *Communication Research, 17*(5), 765-799.

Perse, E. M. (1994). Uses of erotica. *Communication Research, 20*(4), 488-515.

Perse, E. M., & Courtright, J. A. (1993). Normative images of communication media. *Human Communication Review, 19*(4), 485-503.

Perse, E. M., & Rubin, A. L. (1990). Chronic loneliness and television. *Journal of Broadcasting and Electronic Media, 34*(1), 37-53.

Peters, J. D. (1996). The uncanniness of mass communication in interwar social thought. *Journal of Communication, 46*(3), 108-123.

Picard, R. G. (1989). *Media economics.* Newbury Park, CA: Sage.

Pool, I. de Sola, & Shulman, I. (1959). Newsmen's fantasies, audiences, and newswriting. *Public Opinion Quarterly, 23*(2), 145-158.

Radway, J. (1984). *Reading the romance.* Chapel Hill: University of North Carolina Press.

Real, M. (1989). *Supermedia.* Newbury Park, CA: Sage.

Reimer, B. (1994). *The most common of practices: Media use in late modernity.* Stockholm: Almqvist & Wiksell.

Renckstorf, K. (1989). Medienützing als soziales Hendeln. *Kölner Zeitschrift für Soziologie und Sozialpsychologie Sonderheft, 30,* 314-336.

Renckstorf, K., McQuail, D., & Jankowski, N. (Eds.). (1996). *Media use as social action.* London: John Libbey.

Rheingold, H. (1994). *The virtual community.* London: Secker and Warburg.

Rice, R. E. (Ed.). (1984). *The new media.* Beverly Hills, CA: Sage.

Rice, R. E., & Rogers, E. (1980). Reinvention in the innovation process. *Knowledge, 1*(1), 449-514.

Riesman, D., Glazer, N., & Denny, R. (1950). *The lonely crowd.* New Haven, CT: Yale University Press.

Robinson, J., & Levy, M. (1986). *The main source.* Newbury Park, CA: Sage.

Robinson, J. P., & Fink, E. L. (1986). Beyond mass culture and class culture: Subcultural differences in the structure of music preferences. In S. Ball-Rokeach & M. Cantor (Eds.), *Media, audience, and social structure* (pp. 226-239). Newbury Park, CA: Sage.

Roe, K. (1985). Swedish youth and music: Listening patterns and motivation. *Communication Research, 12,* 353-362.

Roe, K. (1992). Different destinies—different melodies: School achievement, anticipated status and adolescents' tastes in music. *European Journal of Communication, 7*(3), 335-358.

Rosen, J., & Merritt, D. (1994). *Public journalism: Theory and practice.* Dayton, OH: Kettering Foundation.

Rosenberg, B., & White, D. M. (Eds.). (1957). *Mass culture.* New York: Free Press.

Rosengren, K. E. (1973). News diffusion: An overview. *Journalism Quarterly, 50,* 83-91.

Rosengren, K. E. (1974). Uses and gratifications: A paradigm outlined. In J. G. Blumler & E. Katz (Eds.), *The uses of mass communications* (pp. 269-286). Beverly Hills, CA: Sage.

Rosengren, K. E., Palmgreen, P., & Rayburn, J. D. (Eds.). (1985). *Media gratification research: Current perspectives.* Beverly Hills, CA: Sage.

Rosengren, K. E., & Windahl, S. (1972). Mass media consumption as a functional alternative. In D. McQuail (Ed.), *Sociology of mass communications* (pp. 166-194). Harmondsworth, UK: Penguin.

Rosengren, K. E., & Windahl, S. (1989). *Media matter: TV use in childhood and adolescence.* Norwood, NJ: Ablex.

Rothenbuhler, E. W. (1987). The living room celebration of the Olympic Games. *Journal of Communication, 38*(4), 61-68.

Rothenbuhler, W., Mullen, L. J., De Carell, R., & Ryan, C. R. (1996). Community, community attachment, and involvement. *Journalism Quarterly, 73*(2), 445-466.

Rubin, A. M. (1983). Television uses and gratifications: The interaction of viewing patterns and motivations. *The Journal of Broadcasting and Electronic Media, 27*(1), 37-51.

Rubin, A. M. (1984). Ritualized and instrumental television viewing. *Journal of Communication, 34*(3), 67-77.

Rubin, A. M., Perse, E. M., & Powell, E. (1989). Loneliness, parasocial interaction and local TV news viewing. *Communication Research, 14,* 246-268.

Ryan, J., & Peterson, R. A. (1982). The product image: The fate of creativity in country music song writing. In J. S. Ettema & D. C. Whitney (Eds.), *Individuals in mass media organizations* (pp. 11-32). Beverly Hills, CA: Sage.

Sabal, R. (1992). Television executives speak about fan letters to the networks. In L. Lewis (Ed.), *The adoring audience* (pp. 185-188). London: Routledge & Kegan Paul.

Saenz, K. (1994). Television as a cultural practice. In H. Newcomb (Ed.), *Television: The critical view* (5th ed., pp. 573-586). New York: Oxford University Press.

Salvaggio, J. L., & Bryant, J. (Eds.). (1989). *Media use in the Information Age.* Hillsdale, NJ: Lawrence Erlbaum.

Schement, J. R., & Curtis, T. (1995). *Tendencies and tensions of the Information Age.* New Brunswick, NJ: Transaction Books.

Schlesinger, P. (1978). *Putting "reality" together: BBC news.* London: Constable.

Schramm, W. (1954). How communication works. In W. Schramm (Ed.), *Process and effects of mass communication* (pp. 3-26). Urbana: University of Illinois Press.

Schramm, W., Lyle, J., & Parker, E. (1961). *Television in the lives of our children.* Stanford, CA: Stanford University Press.

Schrøder, K. C. (1987). Convergence of antagonistic traditions? *European Journal of Communication, 2,* 7-31.

Sears, D. O., & Freedman, J. L. (1971). Selective exposure to information: A critical review. In W. Schramm & D. F. Roberts (Eds.), *The process and effects of mass communication* (pp. 209-234). Urbana: University of Illinois Press.

Seiter, E., Borchers, H., Kreutzner, G., & Warth, E.-M. (Eds.). (1989). *Remote control.* London: Routledge & Kegan Paul.

Sepstrup, P. (1989). Research into international TV flows. *European Journal of Communication, 4*(4), 393-408.

Sepstrup, P. (1990). *The transnationalization of TV in West Europe.* London: John Libbey.

Short, J., Williams, E., & Christie, B. (1976). *The social psychology of telecommunications.* New York: John Wiley.

Signorielli, N., & Morgan, M. (Eds.). (1990). *Cultivation analysis.* Newbury Park, CA: Sage.

Silverstone, R. (1994). *Television and everyday life.* London: Routledge & Kegan Paul.

Singer, B. D. (1973). *Feedback and society.* Lexington, MA: Lexington Books.

Smith, R. (1986). Television addiction. In J. Bryant & D. Zillman (Eds.), *Perspectives on media effects* (pp. 109-128). Hillsdale, NJ: Lawrence Erlbaum.

Smythe, D. W. (1977). Communications: Blindspot of Western Marxism. *Canadian Journal of Political and Social Theory, 1,* 120-127.

Sparks, C., & Campbell, M. (1987). The inscribed reader of the British quality press. *European Journal of Communication, 2*(4), 455-472.

Spears, R., & Lea, M. (1994). Panacea or panopticon? The hidden power in computer-mediated communication. *Communication Research, 21*(4), 427-459.

Stamm, K. R. (1985). *Newspaper use and community ties.* Norwood, NJ: Ablex.

Steiner, G. (1963). *The people look at television.* New York: Knopf.

Tomlinson, J. (1991). *Cultural imperialism.* London: Pinter.

Tuchman, G. (1978). *Making news: A study in the construction of reality.* New York: Free Press.

Tunstall, J. (1971). *Journalists at work.* London: Constable.

Tunstall, J. (1977). *The media are American.* London: Constable.

Twyman, T. (1994). Measuring audiences to radio. In R. Kent (Ed.), *Measuring media audiences* (pp. 88-104). London: Routledge & Kegan Paul.

Van den Bulk, J. (1995). The selective viewer: Defining (Flemish) viewer types. *European Journal of Communication, 10*(2), 147-177.

van Zoonen, E. (1994). *Feminist media theory.* London: Sage.

van Zuylen, J. (1977). *The life-cycle of the family magazine.* Amsterdam: University of Amsterdam Press.

Varis, T. (1984). The international flow of television programs. *Journal of Communication, 34*(1), 143-152.

Waples, D., Berelson, B., & Bradshaw, F. R. (1940). *What reading does to people.* Chicago: University of Chicago Press.

Warner, W. L., & Henry, W. E. (1948). The radio day-time serial: A symbolic analysis. *Genetic Psychology Monographs, 37,* 7-13, 55-64.

Webster, J. G. (1986). Audience behavior in the new media environment. *Journal of Communication, 36*(2), 77-91.

Webster, J. G., & Lichty, L. W. (1991). *Ratings analysis: Theory and practice.* Hillsdale, NJ: Lawrence Erlbaum.

Webster, J. G., & Phalen, P. F. (1994). Victim, consumer, or commodity? Audience models in communication policy. In J. S. Ettema & D. C. Whitney (Eds.), *Audiencemaking: How the media create the audience* (pp. 19-37). Thousand Oaks, CA: Sage.

Webster, J. G., & Phalen, P. F. (1997). *The mass audience: Rediscovering the dominant model.* Mahawa, NJ: Lawrence Erlbaum.

Webster, J. G., & Wakshlag, J. J. (1983). A theory of television program choice. *Communication Research, 10*(4), 430-446.

Weibull, L. (1985). Structural factors in gratifications research. In K. E. Rosengren, P. Palmgreen, & L. Wenner (Eds.), *Media gratifications research: Current perspectives* (pp. 123-147). Beverly Hills, CA: Sage.

Weimann, G., Wober, M., & Brosius, H. (1992). Towards a typology of TV diets. *European Journal of Communication, 7*(4), 491-515.

Westley, B., & MacLean, M. (1957). A conceptual model for mass communication research. *Journalism Quarterly, 34,* 31-38.

Wilson, C. C., & Gutiérrez, F. (1985). *Minorities and the media.* Beverly Hills, CA: Sage.

Wildman, S. (1994). One-way flows and the economics of audience-making. In J. S. Ettema & D. C. Whitney (Eds.), *Audiencemaking: How the media create the audience* (pp. 115-141). Thousand Oaks, CA: Sage.

Williams, R. (1961). *Culture and society 1780-1950.* Harmondsworth, UK: Penguin.

Williams, R. (1974). *Television: Technology and cultural form.* London: Fontana.

Windahl, S., Signitzer, B., & Olson, J. (1992). *Using communication theory.* Newbury Park, CA: Sage.

Winston, B. (1986). *Misunderstanding media.* Cambridge, MA: Harvard University Press.

Wright, C. R. (1974). Functional analysis and mass communication revisited. In J. G. Blumler & E. Katz (Eds.), *The uses of mass communications* (pp. 197-212). Beverly Hills, CA: Sage.

Zillman, D. (1980). The anatomy of suspense. In P. H. Tannenbaum (Ed.), *The entertainment functions of television* (pp. 133-163). Hillsdale, NJ: Lawrence Erlbaum.

Zillman, D. (1985). The experimental explorations of gratifications from media entertainment. In D. Zillman & J. Bryant (Eds.), *Selective exposure to communication* (pp. 225-239). Hillsdale, NJ: Lawrence Erlbaum.

Zillman, D., & Bryant, J. (Eds.). (1985). *Selective exposure to communication.* Hillsdale, NJ: Lawrence Erlbaum.

Index

Active audience, 22-3, 58-62, 71, 72, 85, 149
Advertising, 5, 13, 14, 17, 22, 27, 33-34, 42, 44,
    57, 58, 65, 114, 116, 124, 130, 141, 148
Alasuutari, P., 96, 106
Ang, I., 12, 13, 14, 20, 29, 43, 97, 106, 136
Attention model, 40-42
Audience:
    attitudes to communicators, 118-119
    as commodity, 14, 23, 35, 122
    as market, 8-9, 131
    as spectators, 35, 41-42, 44
    collective aspect of, 3-4, 10, 24, 90-91, 121,
        134
    concept, 1-2, 23, 26-32, 37-40, 142-3,
        148-150
    cumulation, 83
    discourse, 32
    feedback, 79, 110-112, 113
    fragmentation, 55, 132-133, 137-138, 143
    homogeneity, 10, 55, 146

    inheritance, 62
    loyalty, 66, 82-84, 134-135
    needs, 26-55
    participation, 117-118, 123
    perceptions of, 12, 42, 112-116
    ratings, 14, 34-35, 54, 57-8, 61, 110, 114
    repeat viewing, 82-83
    research, 11, 15-16, 21, 34, 65-67, 87-88,
        95, 111
Audiencehood, 20, 88, 90-91, 97
Avery, R., 29, 92, 124

Barwise, P., 17, 58, 83, 103, 105
Bauer, R., 59, 113
Berelson, B., 18, 70
Biltereyst, D., 107, 137, 140
Biocca, F., 2, 44, 59
Blumer, H., 6, 18
Blumler, J. G., 18, 32, 40, 71, 72, 75, 124

About the Author

Denis McQuail is now Professor Emeritus of Communication at the University of Amsterdam, The Netherlands, and Visiting Professor at the University of Southampton, England. His teaching career was spent largely at these universities. His first degree was in history, at Oxford University, and his PhD is from Leeds University. He holds an Honorary Doctorate from the University of Ghent. He has held a number of visiting positions, including posts at the University of Pennsylvania, Columbia University, Harvard University, Moscow University, and Tampere University. His career has been spent in teaching and research in relation to mass media, with particular reference to the role of mass media in election campaigns, audience research, media policy, and mass communication theory. He has published a number of books, most recently *Media Performance* (1992), *Communication Models* (with Sven Windahl, revised edition, 1993), and a new (third) edition of *Mass Communication Theory*. These and earlier books have been translated into a number of languages and widely used in teaching.

Denis McQuail is a member of the Euromedia Research Group and editor of the *European Journal of Communication*. He is a staff member of the Amsterdam School of Communication Research. His current research centers on comparative media policy and questions of media accountability.